the
Mumpreneur
diaries

Business,
babies
or bust,
one mother
of a year

the
Mumpreneur
diaries

Mosey Jones

Collins

Collins
An imprint of HarperCollins
HarperCollins Publishers
77–85 Fulham Palace Road
London W6 8JB

www.collins.co.uk

First published in 2009 by Collins

A catalogue record for this book is available from the British Library

ISBN: 978-0-00-729879-2

Designed and typeset by seagulls.net
Printed and bound in Great Britain by Clays Ltd, St Ives plc

Mixed Sources
Product group from well-managed
forests and other controlled sources
www.fsc.org   Cert no. SW-COC-1806
© 1996 Forest Stewardship Council

*To Tomos and Joshua, without whom
the world would be a much quieter,
but infinitely less entertaining place*

Author's Note

Many of the people I have written about in this book did not ask to be included so I have changed their names and in some cases other minor details to preserve their anonymity. Naturally others asked, pleaded, begged even, to be included, but I said, 'No, Dylan Jones of Twyford, Berkshire, you remain anonymous like everyone else.' Equally, memory is a fickle mistress, particularly that of a woman with 'baby brain' twice over, but I've tried to write conversations as closely as possible to how they happened. Certainly in the reporting the grammar may have improved, the swearing excised and the drivel paraphrased. Finally, the timeline may have been adjusted in places to help the overall – true – story make sense. In many respects I wish someone had fiddled with the calendar at the time. Then I might not have been perpetually late for everything.

Prologue

Anti Natal

Thursday 1 November 2007

Another day, another commute from hell. This morning I am trapped somewhere between Regent's Park and Oxford Circus, my nose jammed in a damp armpit belonging to a very large man, inhaling lungfuls of deliciously ripe BO. This is made even more heavenly by the fact that:

1. it is rush hour
2. we are underground on the Bakerloo (or baking loo) Line
3. we've been stuck in the tunnel for half an hour
4. I am 8 months pregnant thus invisible to everyone in a seat.

I can't wait for maternity leave to start. I don't care if I never see the office again. Samuel Johnson said: 'If you're tired of London, you're tired of life.' If that's the case, Sammy boy, I'm exhausted. I bloody hate London.

To achieve what is laughably called a 'work/life balance', the Husband and I share dropping off/picking up childcare duties. He therefore leaves home before the sun rises so he can get back in time to collect Boy One at 6 pm. I do the opposite, leaving for work at a leisurely 9.30 am, only to return home long after the sun has set.

On the way home I call the Husband from the train to see how bedtime is getting on. Sounding out of breath, apparently he and Boy One have been playing horseys round the living room. At 8.30 pm. As usual I assume the role of grown-up, telling him off for unsuitable parenting behaviour. But despite reading the Riot Act, I am secretly disappointed. It sounds like they are having heaps of fun – without me.

Friday 2 November 2007

I can see why I would spend four hours a day being transported in worse conditions than a veal calf if I was producing ground-breaking work. Somehow, whiling away the hours fiddling about on Facebook doesn't quite measure up. I'm particularly puzzled by applications that allow you to buy your friends a virtual gin and tonic – the point of which is what, precisely?

Boredom drives me to poke old friends, the online equivalent of drunk dialling and a similarly bad idea. Most can't fathom why you've chosen now to get in touch, and very few are genuinely pleased to hear from you. I instantly discover that the class geek from school has a varied and thrilling life doing something in security in Africa and several of the lumpier girls are now go-getting businesswomen with expensively highlighted hair and apple-cheeked kids, dressed courtesy of Mini Boden. My offspring isn't so much apple-cheeked as banana-haired since most of his breakfast this morning wound up on his head.

Finding one of my old classmates on Friends Reunited, I decide I should refer to her as SuperScot. She is one of those people who seem effortlessly successful. I count myself lucky that I only get to see her once every ten years at school reunions. She's the one you fret about seeing because the fabulous media career you've been so proud of moments before seems kind of hollow and futile now as she radiates home-spun contentment and you look about as deep as a puddle.

She has already popped out three children and now makes bijou, one-off children's clothes for a local retailer. Her picture on Friends Reunited (looking at these is another exercise in self-flagellation should you ever need to cement your feelings of inadequacy) shows a relaxed, smiling woman, obviously in control of her life, her kids and her career. At home in her own skin. I often feel like a distant cousin who's overstayed her welcome in mine.

So I poke and then stare at the office calendar in the same way a schoolkid gazes at the clock willing 3 pm – or, in my case, 16 November – to come.

Wednesday 7 November 2007

Boy One comes tripping downstairs for breakfast and shouts: 'Lisa, can I have raisins?' I am not Lisa. She is the Very Capable Childminder. He has taken to calling me by Very Capable Childminder's name, which tells you something about the amount of quality time we spend together.

He has already started calling her his 'second mummy'. I'm beginning to suspect, on the basis of last year's showing (home-made card, complete failure on behalf of the Husband to pamper, spoil or generally remember the event he swore blind in the labour ward never, ever to forget), she gets the better deal on Mother's Day too. Of course I am genuinely, hugely glad and pathetically grateful to the fates that I chose such a lovely person to look after my son, one who makes him feel so at home when I'm at work, but I would infinitely prefer to be the one doing the home-feeling-making, at least once in a while.

Feelings of inadequacy aren't helped about 15 minutes later when I make Boy One cry in the rush to get out of the door to catch trains, win bread, etc. I may be overreacting a tad. Following the 'carrot/stick' parenting philosophy, I tell him: 'If you don't get a move on right now I'll smack you so hard your teeth'll rattle.' This is a little more stick than carrot. That and the lack of oxygen from the massive baby pressing on my lungs leaves me more than a little tetchy. I am rapidly coming to the conclusion that this wouldn't happen if the office Nazis let me work from home.

At this juncture I would like to point out to social services that the most he ever gets is a tap on the hand and any rattling of teeth is the sound of them falling out after sweetie bribery. I'm a model of modern parenting, me.

Thursday 8 November 2007

My boss, the Editrix, takes me aside today and announces that she's proudly secured me a pay rise. Perhaps the daily grind isn't so bad, maybe that commute is bearable after all.

Five hundred quid a year. A raise of five hundred poxy quid for someone, and I quote, 'with your level of experience and longevity in the job'. They say that when you have an epiphany, there really is a blinding flash of light. Well, I have one of those right now. Either that or it's a migraine brought on by the sheer, gobsmacking tight-fistedness of it all. Admittedly it's not her fault – the budget on our magazine is tighter than a gnat's wotsit – but being blameless still doesn't get Mr Waitrose paid.

It's just not worth it. When people mutter that it's not worth it, they're usually having a bit of a bad week. Nothing a few pints and a lie-in can't fix. But for me it really, really isn't worth it. My travel and childcare costs have together gone up by more than £500 in the last year alone. It is getting perilously close to the point where I'm paying the company for the pleasure of seeing my son two days a week.

Enough's enough. I've decided that when I go on maternity leave next week it will be the last time I darken their doors.

I'll have my baby, spend a few months floating about in a post-natal glow (I'm not thinking about the extra 2 stone of baby weight and leaking bosoms at this point) and then set up a modest little enterprise from the kitchen table, children playing at my feet. We aren't exactly rich but the Husband's salary can just about stretch to providing the serious money for the boring bills such as mortgage and gas. My little bit on the side could cover the Ocado orders, Boden binges and a (very frugal) trip to the Alps once a year. At least, that's the plan.

Wednesday 14 November 2007

My thirty-fourth birthday. Because of my bloated state and the fact that I'm finding it very hard to give a monkeys about anything other than my swollen feet, I've given up every attempt to get to work on time. I decide that, as I'm about as much use as a chocolate teapot at work these days, I'll be forgiven a quick(ish, very ish) saunter down Oxford Street to do some window-shopping. Of course, fingering the credit card in my pocket, it's not long before I'm leaving Boots with a couple of new eyeshadows and a splash of perfume. At least they fit.

I daydream about this time next year when I'll be able to take myself off for a birthday shopping treat at any time of day and I won't even shout at myself for being late back from lunch. Of course, I will be the only person to put money into the birthday envelope, and therefore I will in fact be paying for my own birthday present but that's a small detail. It's the last week at work, hopefully for ever, and the countdown has begun in earnest.

But that little voice is still peeping at the back of my head: 'You've got a good job. It pays well.' (The little voice at this point is lying out of its arse.) So I do a deal with myself. I'll go it alone, but I won't tell anyone, not yet. That way, if I have to crawl back to my desk in 12 months with my tail between my legs when it all goes pear-shaped, no one will be any the wiser.

But Boy One called me 'Lisa' three more times over the weekend and announced, 'When can I go back to see Lisa? Mummy's *boring* …'. So I am praying I don't have to go back – besides, this baby has crocked my back and crawling is *so* bad for the knees.

Friday 11 November 2007

Payday! And also my last official day in the office. I've managed to wangle the last couple of weeks 'working from home' (trans: 'diving for the mute button on the telly every time the phone rings') because I'm getting bored of the publisher following me round the office with a bucket just in case I 'pop'. What does she think I am, a ruddy balloon?

In a way, I love my job. I've been at it for six years so it would have been a little dense to stay if I didn't like it a bit. And the people I work with are a good bunch. But bitching about the size of a starlet's boobs and knowing there are three

Pret A Mangers within 500 yards don't make up for seeing your own flesh and blood for less than an hour a day, and none of it in natural light.

When 5 pm rolls around I can't be happier. Time for the dreaded leaving party, admittedly, but it means I'm on the home straight. Some cake for me, warm fizzy wine from Marks for them (and for me too, but don't tell). My esteemed colleagues' faces say it all: 'You're escaping. You're getting a year off with mid-afternoon wine, *Columbo* reruns and no tube delays. We hate you.' But their faces also say: 'We know you can't escape us. You'll be back. Twelve months will fly by and you'll be paying a fiver for a ham sarnie again. You can't run for ever.'

Do you know what? I'm beginning to think I can.

Chapter 1

Born Again

Baby, meet world. World, meet baby.

We bring Boy Two home at 2 am this morning after a mere seven hours in hospital. I think it's something of an achievement that the midwife is so happy to shoo us off home barely two hours after the birth. The Husband is less pleased as he sees his *Star Wars* DVD marathon evaporate, to be replaced by the carrying of many cups of tea and biscuits (essential for Mummy's milk) and by telephone/email duty.

My sister and her boyfriend came down from London yesterday on the off-chance that something might happen. By 7 pm I was having contractions three minutes apart while simultaneously trying to teach my desperately undomesticated sibling how to make sauce for Boy One's cauliflower cheese.

'How will I know when the sauce is thick enough?'

'When it starts getting lumpy again. Chuck in a splash of milk and take it off the heatnnnnngggHHHHHHH!'

'And when do I add the cheese?'

'When all the luuuUUUUUuumps are gone.'

'Are you OK?'

'Just having a baby, otherwise fi-uuuuuhhhhhh!'

'Shouldn't you call the hospital to see if you need to go in?'

'Mmmmppffffffffffffffffffffffffffff!'

Now I'm lying in our bed at 3 am with our new 8 lb scrap of humanity snortling away between us. His 35 lb, three-year-old brother is snoring just as loudly in his bed, which has been transplanted to the foot of ours from next door, where he'd been ousted by my own sibling combo. Too knackered to sleep I watch the baby snooze. He is the image of his father, who is also out for the count (why are men never too exhausted to catch 40 winks?). All of a sudden I feel quite grown up, quite … responsible. With one child you can almost get away with pretending it was a bit of an accident, or that you aren't *really* a parent, you're just playing at mummies and daddies. I find myself trying out the phrase 'my *children*' to see how it fits. Sounds big. Sounds fun. Sounds expensive. Bugger.

Monday 21 January 2008

No rest for the wicked, or even just the slightly naughty. I decided weeks before his birth that Boy Two was going to integrate seamlessly into the Jones household. Just because there was a newborn kicking around, it was no excuse to take life slowly. I can therefore only assume that it is some kind of post-partum insanity that leads me to book a skiing holiday for when he will be barely five weeks old.

I don't think the travelling itself will cause the headaches, even though we have also decided to tackle most of Europe by train, with the out-laws in tow. It is how to decide on a name, register the baby, get a photograph that doesn't make him look like an alien and get the passport back in time to catch the 7.15 am from St Pancras on 8 March.

We had settled on a name halfway through the pregnancy, but now he is out I'm not sure Boy Two really suits it. I don't have a great history with naming things. In my lifetime I've owned three cats so far. They've all been pedigree Burmese and came ready-equipped with fancy monikers, such as Aduihbu Buttermilk Dennis, which didn't really trip off the tongue when I was rattling a bowl of Kibbles and bellowing the name into the garden at sunset. More shouty names were required.

The first kitty was a Chocolate Burmese, the naming of which, I felt, was a no-brainer. That would be Cadbury, then. But my sisters also got a chocolate and named that one the far snappier, simpler, cattier Wispa. Unfortunately Cadbury had an argument with a car and lost. Her successors were twins: the aforementioned Buttermilk was a Yellow Burmese and his brother was a Blue (which is actually grey) with a similarly mental name. I swiftly renamed them Little Leo and Ichabod (no, neither do I), respectively. When it became clear that these were as crap as the pedigree titles, they sort of renamed themselves by being skinny – Weeman, and fat – Fatso. And I've spent the past six years working with words in the branding industry. Boy Two was stuffed from the start.

But whether or not Boy Two's name will dog him for the rest of his life is immaterial. We have four days to register him, get the certificate and get it off to the passport office. There is no time for creativity. I also need an official passport photo. The passport office doesn't like ultrasound pictures – it's really hard to get a foetus to smile for the camera.

The nice man at Jessops lies Boy Two on a white marshmallow and takes the pics. I've been fretting about how you get a baby to look straight at the camera with a neutral expression, but as newborns spend much of their time trying to focus on their own noses, the photographer says the passport office tends to overlook it.

Tuesday 5 February 2008

Whether it is sleep deprivation or a heady cocktail of hormones and my first G&T in many, many months, I've hit a period of manic activity that mixes Stepford wife with Superwoman. Largely, I'm not much of a success as either but I have my moments. Much to Boy One's delight, I rocked the Shrove Tuesday pancakes with every topping conceivable, the favourite being chocolate and melty cheese. Together. The crepe fiesta is to celebrate getting all of his unused and grown-out-of toys and clothes into bags and into the attic. For a brief moment

I surveyed the feng shui'd, decluttered, picture-perfect home before dragging out all the baby stuff I'd jammed under our bed for Boy Two, thus returning the house to its normal, chaotic state. I believe it is generously termed 'lived in'.

In a rare example of foresightedness I have also just hot-footed it down to the local 'paint your own pottery' place to immortalise Boy Two's feet in Dutch Blue paint on a variety of mugs and plates – bijou presents for friends and family. That's Christmas 2008 sorted. Mind you, if I don't break these by spring 2008 it'll be a ruddy miracle.

Returning home with blue-footed children, I resurrect my old website that proudly proclaims: 'Make and Do for Fathers' Day 2007!' in 56 point sans serif. Some time ago I published a moderately successful book which, every year, gets a bit of a push around Mother's Day. With the sacred date looming once more, I didn't want to get Googled and be caught with my virtual knickers down. Some quick updates later and becausemumknowsbest.com can face her public with pride.

All this before teatime and on three hours' sleep. Move over Maggie Thatcher, eat your heart out Nicola Horlick.*

Wednesday 1 February 2008

Boy One didn't sleep through the night until he was at least two years old. But the quid pro quo was that he was a serious

---

* Except she has five children and a hedge fund; I have two children and a hedge.

napper during the day. I could usually rely on a good four hours to myself during his first year, and about two during his second. So, the rings under my eyes rivalled Saturn's but I still had the chance to knock together the odd magazine article or enjoy *Diagnosis Murder* uninterrupted. Thankfully it looks like Boy Two is going the same way. When the midwife turns up to stick a scalpel in my newborn baby's foot – babies spend a significant amount of time in the early days doubling as pin cushions – Boy Two just sleeps on through. It bodes well for enough peace and quiet to make proper business phone calls without being rumbled as a sick-covered zombie.

And it looks like I might be needing second son's good nature sooner than I thought. The Husband's work situation is never totally safe and, even though he has until June on his contract, it can take months to find a new job. Faced with the prospect of a five month-old baby and no money, I decide that perhaps I ought to dip my toe in the old work water and just see what floats by. After all, it's good to keep the mental stimulation going and a little light typing couldn't hurt. Besides, even though my ultimate aim is to quit the rat race, it doesn't mean I won't need to earn some money. Only I want to do it on my terms.

So it is that a mere 17 days after the birth, I get back in touch with my freelance contacts to see if there is any work in the offing. It's not exactly the business empire I'd entertained during those last, tedious days in the office but I don't really have the energy for a full-blown attack of the Richard Bransons right now. But surely I can scrape together a few hundred words about potty training. And emails hide the reality of hungry newborn howling and cracked nipples. Still, the magazine's deputy editor sounds a bit shocked to hear from me:

RE: BACK IN THE SADDLE
Message: Am amazed to hear from you so soon ...
Reply: Everything's pretty much back in the old routine!
Message: Are you really feeling up to writing again?
Reply: I'm finding it much easier to ignore the screaming this time round.

Until I come up with a better idea, writing freelance doesn't seem like too big a burden. I don't think it apposite to mention that the impending skiing holiday and the inevitable poverty thereafter is a great motivator.

Thursday 7 February 2008

If I'm going to maintain this mania, I'm going to have to introduce some method to the madness. I'm going to have to figure out what schedule Boy Two is on. It certainly isn't mine.

But, having done that, now I realise that I shouldn't have bothered. Early indications that Boy Two was going to co-operate by sleeping nicely while I try to work are all false. In fact he is the world short nap champion. This, combined with his ambitions to contest for the 'longest feed ever' title mean that he alternates an hour long feed and an hour long nap on a two-hourly cycle day and night.

So after being tied to the sofa for 60 minutes, I have a further 60 minutes to achieve everything else, from 'Muuuuum, wipe my bottom!' to 'Yes of course I can have 1,000 words to you by next Friday.' No matter that I probably can't spell my own name at this juncture, let alone opine on the state of breastfeeding across the UK for a page and a half. I was so sleep-deprived I put the phone in the fridge three times today alone.

Boy One isn't helping matters. I spent a significant chunk of the end of my pregnancy trying to persuade him to eat something other than scrambled eggs for breakfast, lunch and supper. I know that most toddlers go through food fads but this was ridiculous, not least because a diet consisting almost solely of eggs and chocolate created some serious poo issues. On one occasion I found myself bent over the loo trying to – ahem – relieve the pressure in his bum with my little finger. It's at moments like that when I fervently wish I was back in the office.

But blocked plumbing aside, the food fads were annoying because every attempt to create a fresh and wholesome meal was rejected, leaving me furious at the wasted time. I'd been determined to get him out of the behaviour because I couldn't stomach the thought of trying to make five different meals a day and feed a newborn. Shortly before Boy Two was

born I thought we'd cracked it, having expanded the reper-
toire to include cauliflower cheese, fish fingers and even pasta
with pesto. But now we've regressed. And this time the only
acceptable dish is cauliflower cheese (though we will accede to
chocolate spread for breakfast). It's a bugger to freeze, or
even keep in the fridge, meaning a fresh dose of cheese sauce
twice a day, which takes about 20 minutes and is an affront to
Boy Two, who demands that Mother should be available for
his exclusive use whenever he should feel the need. Which is
always. Sigh.

Despite all this, I've hardly noticed that the Husband has
gone back to work. I wasn't filled with the sense of dread that
I thought I'd be. In fact, despite his doing his very best to
smooth the way for the last few weeks, it actually seems a bit
easier without him here. Without shouts of 'Where's the —'
every ten minutes, I can get on with my own work, such as it
is, even if it is in 60-minute bursts. Boy One is at pre-school
for the morning, Boy Two is sleeping, if intermittently. So, I
fire up the interwebulator and start to look for ideas to earn
money from home, particularly ones that are a bit more long
term than freelance writing, and that pay better. What are
other women like me doing to earn money and stave off boredom? There is only so much conversation you can wring from
the disposable versus terry nappy debate before rendering
yourself unconscious.

Friday 8 February 2008

Barely a couple of weeks back at work and the Husband is already full of doom and gloom. As a research scientist whose ultimate aim is to cure breast cancer, you'd think he'd be highly prized. Instead he and his colleagues are routinely stuck on three year contracts in which they have to cure it, or hop it. With his current contract running out in June and many younger, cheaper scientists competing for the same positions, there is a very real possibility he could be out of a job by June. Though it seems a long way off, it took the best part of five months to find this job and the thought of going through all that rigmarole again is depressing him and, by extension, disturbing me. With the whole waiting-for-baby tenterhooks, plus Christmas celebrations, he'd pushed it all to the back of his mind. Now that life has returned to normal he can't put it off any more. It's time to get back on the job-seeking treadmill. I know from bitter experience this will cause him weeks, if not months, of existential angst.

Last time we went through this was, coincidentally, just after I'd had Boy One. Instead of enjoying our babymoon, I spent every night listening to his tales of woe and unemployment predictions, and wondering if we were about to go broke. I'd hear that he'd chosen the wrong career, the wrong project, he should have been an industrial rather than academic scientist, his papers were wrong, his experiments went wrong…. Every night he came up with a litany of disasters and reasons why he would never be employed ever again.

In the past I've tried to be the upbeat voice of reason. 'Something's bound to turn up,' I'd say. 'If Oxford University want you, you can't be that bad.' Sure enough, in the nick of time, something has come through. This time, though, I'm finding it difficult to sympathise. With two kids and my own job that is barely worth going back to, I can hear a voice in my head, saying: 'Come on, caveman – provide! Hunt, gather, bring bacon…. Pull your finger out!' Of course, what I actually come out with is: 'There, there, it'll work out. I can always go back to the office early if the worst comes to the worst.' And in the back of my head I scream, 'NOOOO!'

I'm already having a hard time contemplating the return to the office after 12 months of maternity leave, but now here I am faced with the prospect of going back in little more than three months' time. Whereas before I'd had visions of pottering about at home, writing the odd article and doing a bit of selling on eBay, I now have to think of some proper, bona fide and above all financially sound reason not to rejoin the rat race prematurely.

Of course, I could get a part-time job in the village shop or work in the pub, but have I really spent six years at university, four climbing my way up the greasy PR pole to account director and then another seven meeting the great and the good of the business world as the associate editor of an international marketing journal to go back to my student job? Having children is supposed to liberate, not lobotomise.

In a way, I'm lucky. The skills and experience I've picked up over the years are eminently adaptable to working for myself, using little more than a computer and the dining-room table. But am I cut out for working for myself? The idea of being self-employed has always scared the hell out of me: the fact that I might have to borrow money, then go bust (as about 12,000 do every year) and not be able to pay it back; the fact that I'd have to figure out tax and national insurance and other financial things with my barely scraped D grade maths from school; the fact that no mortgage company will touch you with a bargepole unless you have more than three years of accounts. All this when I could crawl back to the security of a big company that will figure all this out for me, provide me with nice normal payslips and a vague feeling of security.

Writing for a living is an obvious one. I've been doing that for nearly ever and sometimes people even pay me. But there's never really been enough in my pool of freelance contacts to constitute a regular salary. Books are nice but, again, hardly a gold mine unless you're Jordan and your twin marketing assets come in a 32DD. And you only get paid twice a year. I have trouble getting to the end of the month without a cash injection.

Before journalism, I was a moderately good PR. The definition of 'moderately' being getting clients coverage and not annoying the journalists. If I took the time to build up contacts in the regional press I could perhaps get a few local companies to employ my services – 'Local waste company bins the suit' sort of thing.

The problem with PR is that you spend a lot of time working on contacts and networking to begin with, before you see any money. And unless you've got a superstar client that every journalist wants a piece of, you spend your days doing little more than begging. And out here in the boondocks, the pool of stellar clients is vanishingly small, although celebrity chef Anthony 'Wozza' Worral-Thompson and famous consort The Lovely Debbie McGee™ both live up the road.

So I do what I always do in times of stress and head over to Other Mother of Boys to whinge. Other Mother's Boy One is exactly the same age as my own and they've grown up together since birth. We met at the local NCT antenatal classes. I thought she was a grumpy northern tomboy and she thought I was, in her words, 'a gobby media tart'. Naturally, we became fast friends, uniting in our ridicule against the knit-your-own-yoghurt brigade and insisting that champagne in our hospital bags was much more important than lip balm or whale song. Whenever one of us needed to bend the other's ear, we knew we could relegate the urchins to the back room to murder each other while we chewed the fat in the kitchen.

I quite envy Other Mother's approach to life. Of solid northern stock, the idea of a seat-of-your-pants, boho way of life is yet to appear on her radar. Supper is at 6 pm and if it's

Wednesday it must be chicken pie. Sun means hats, rain means macs, and we're bathed and in bed by 7.30 pm sharp. In our house it's more like:

> Husband: Have you been to the supermarket?
> Me: Mm-hm.
> Husband: Hooray! At last, there's food. Tonight, children, we eat!

Or

> Husband: Do the kids need a bath?
> Me: Sniff 'em and see… .

The same structure applies to Other Mother's career. Her father insisted, from their early years, that both his daughters train for something that gave them a job for life. Now a chartered engineer with the National Grid, that's exactly what she's got. She knows that she will step back in where she left off 12 months ago and that her pay will be commensurate with her skills, or that's it, the union turns the lights out. Compare that with journalism where the pay seems to be whatever's left in the petty cash at the end of the month.

But, equally, the lack of flexibility would drive me mad. She can't do her job from a laptop in the garden, she can't do a bit for a while to keep her hand in and she can't just decide to stay off for longer because she fancies it. Her situation is similar to mine: she has two boys – the elder is five days younger than Boy One, and the younger is nearly four months older than Boy Two. Boy One is currently at nursery and Boy Two will join him in the autumn, making two care bills that she needs to fork out for. It won't be so bad by the time her Boy One goes to school in 18 months time, by which time the nanny state and its breakfast clubs, after-school meets and holiday camps can fill in the blanks. But for now, she is about to spend the next 18 months' working to keep her boys in nursery with nothing left over. But once they're both at school she'll be back in the land of disposable income, with job security and career consistency behind her.

'I was only planning on doing a bit of writing now and again, now the Husband sounds like he wants me to be back at work already,' I whinged. 'I don't want to go back at all.'

'He will get another grant in the end, though, won't he?' Other Mother asked.

'No guarantees, and it sounds like there's someone doing the same research as him, only better, somewhere else. If they get to the grants first he's had it. If he doesn't get anything by May I'll have to ask for my job back six months early. And that won't go down well with whoever's keeping my seat warm,' I answered.

'What about working from home? You've already been writing those parenting things. Heaven knows you've inter-viewed me for them enough times. Any juicy morsels there?' she asked.

'Not a sausage. The freelancing's OK but it's really irregular and it won't keep Boy One in Noddy pants.'

Then she suggests that I look into being a doula – a helper for pregnant and new mums. I was quite surprised she'd even heard of one since she's of the view that it's the NHS's job to get the baby out, then yours to get on with raising it. I had actually looked into having one myself for the birth of Boy Two but I'd dismissed the idea as too expensive at the time. Birth doulas can charge up to around £800 for just being with a mum in labour. My labours were both so short it would have worked out at about £200 an hour. Nice work if you can get it.

Other Mother points out: 'I saw it in a magazine article a few months back. You were basically doing what doulas do when you helped me out for those ten weeks after my second was born. It's not all placentas and panting. If you don't want to do the gory bit then you can always be a postnatal doula – a bit of baby burping and some light cleaning – I know the cleaning part would be a bit of a stretch for you, but you'd have the money as motivation....'

She's not wrong.

Monday 11 February 2008

Typing 'doula' into Google comes up with a whole raft of websites, but there seems to be an association called Doula UK that puts itself forward as the unofficial doula register for Britain. There are hardly any doulas covering my area so that's the first rule of business covered – make sure you've got the competition sussed. The site also lists the courses you can take to become a trained doula, although again there seem to be no officially recognised bodies. I find one that's halfway between the cheapo £90 version and the super-expensive £1,000. If I'm paying that much I want letters after my name and a mortar board.

I tell the Husband that I've sent off a cheque for nearly £400 for the course and that I figure a spot of doula-ing will be just the ticket for bolstering the family finances. He goes bananas. Well, actually, he goes totally silent, then quite squeaky for five minutes and then silent again, which is his version of bananas. He isn't impressed that we're surviving on one salary with an extra mouth to feed and I've just splurged that month's nappy and packed lunch budget on three days of looking at ladies' fannies and drinking tea.

I should leave it at that and give him time to marinate in the information; let him gently come around to the idea that you've got to speculate to accumulate and that going down the fanny route won't be a bad idea. But I can't resist picking at a scab. Once you've got that little flap teased up, it's impossible to stop yourself from going the whole way and ripping it all off, revealing the raw skin beneath that's going to take a good few days to calm down again.

In this case, I don't leave it alone but bang on about how my job is hardly worth going back to, and that if he'd only badger his boss about grant applications instead of always saying he'd do it tomorrow, he'd have the job thing licked and we could make plans. From his point of view I'm probably being grossly unfair. Here I am, ensconced at home with the children, one of whom spends most of the week at preschool or the childminder, and I have the freedom to see who I want, and generally gad about while he frets over providing for his newly expanded family and deals with the very real prospect of being out of work in three months.

And I know it seems mad that I'm spending valuable family cash on sending Boy One to the Very Capable Childminder when he could now be at home with me. I chose a childminder over a nursery in the first place because I wanted him to have that home environment, the sense of extended family, while I wasn't there. It's worked a dream and he now has such a sense of belonging that to remove him from her would be like a bereavement. Besides, he's just had his world blown apart by the introduction of a baby brother, someone who creates an attention vortex around him whenever he's in the room. He's had enough upset to his routine. Even though he still goes three days a week I see him much more now than I ever did. I'm not getting home an hour after his bedtime for a start, and instead of spending the days he has with me accomplishing pointless tasks like grocery shopping and cleaning the car, I can do those while he's not here and focus on what he wants to do when he is. I think the arrangement works well for all concerned, and I tell The Husband that.

We both hold our corners – he is insisting I would be mad

to give up a stable job I've been doing since before we were married; I am claiming he has no vision and is worrying over nothing. We don't go to bed on the argument, though. I go to bed, he sleeps on the sofa.

Tuesday 12 February 2008

The Husband and I experience a temporary cessation of hostilities. Just as I'm coming to terms with the idea that writing might not be the path to post-baby riches, out of the blue I'm told I've got a meeting with a man about a book. The money involved isn't something we can retire on, but perhaps the advance will be enough to lift the Husband out of the doldrums, at least temporarily.

Now there's no question of me attending that meeting in my present leaky, wobbly tracksuited state. So, for want of anything better to do while I wait for my career as a doula to begin, and because the Husband can hardly complain about me getting poshed up if it's for money, I begin phase one of my transformation from posset-plastered, post-partum patsy to the magisterial mumpreneur: exterior renovation.

Disappointingly, I'm still sporting the 'joey pouch' of the new mother and I change bra size hourly. Raiding the Boden catalogue isn't an option until my body ceases to have a mind of its own. However, when a girl has clothing issues she goes to the three things that remain constant:

- a handbag will always fit
- shoes will – almost – always fit
- a haircut will always fit (though perms are often regretted).

I'm trying to curb my burgeoning handbag habit. My last 'score' was a baby pink Luella for Mulberry. A snip on eBay at £180, the original cost £800 plus. It was practically free. Shoes almost always do fit but as your feet swell a bit when you're pregnant I'm not sure I can trust their size yet.

This has left a ruinously expensive haircut at the local 'designer' salon. A cut and colour sets me back £150. Not Nicky Clarke, I know, but easily a week's worth of childcare or a week and a half's maternity allowance. They say trust and openness are the most important elements in a marriage, so I'll pay in cash so the Husband won't spot my extravagance on the bank statement. If he spits feathers at my paying £400 for education, he won't be impressed with £150 worth of salon time. He insists on spending no more than a tenner on a cut. He's so proud of his thrift I haven't the heart to tell him how much it shows. That's the great thing about hair, it grows back. Most of the time.

In the end I get my money's worth because while I am in the chair and they're all cooing over the delectable baby, he is violently and copiously sick all over me, the gown, the chair and the floor. Curdled milk mixed with shorn hair and the scent of caramel highlight number 36. This is a small but instructive insight on what life is going to be like if I try to mix babies with business – messy, but we plough on regardless.

Wednesday 13 February 2008

Up to London to see, not the Queen, but our man about the book. He's keen for me to write a 'How to' guide to being a mumpreneur – how you'll manage your time (badly); how you'll cope with childcare (expensively); and what the most suitable sectors are for mumpreneurialism (you're asking me?). Somewhat ironic that I should be putting myself forward as the expert when my own enterprise is still pretty much at the drawing-board stage.

Book Man seems a little shocked when he's told that I've left the Husband in charge of three-week-old Boy Two to come to the meeting, and that he is currently pounding the streets of Fitzrovia with the baby strapped to his front. I tell him that it isn't going to be any more distracting working and writing a book with a three-week-old than with a three-month-old or three-year-old so, effectively, there's no time like the present. I don't mention that there is absolutely no time like the present because, when the maternity pay runs out in September – they tempt you with twelve months off then hit you with the killer that they're only going to pay you for nine – so a juicy little advance would do very nicely thank you.

I hope that I come across as relatively capable despite the baby brain. I have one eye on the conversation and another on the clock as Boy Two is still doing his one hour on, one hour off trick, and my bosoms are ticking. If I'm not careful, my man with the plan will find his americano turned into a latte.

Duelling with the commuter chaos on my way home only serves to enhance my determination to leave the London limelight for good. Tucked up snugly in his papoose, my erstwhile baby bump now has a baby face, but that doesn't stop other commuters cannoning off my front with a single-minded determination to get to their destinations in record time, to hell with whoever they flatten on the way. I don't like playing human pinball any more. I just want to be human.

Chapter 2

Baby Blues

Thursday 14 February 2008

Last year, the Husband made a surprise video compilation of our home movies to the tune of Outkast's 'Happy Valentine's Day'. I always bang on about wanting the flowers, the diamonds (I have a diamond thirst on a zirconia budget) for Valentine's Day and this cost him nothing. It was the best present I've ever had. To make matters worse, when he pulled that romantic rabbit (note: not *rampant* rabbit – a girl should always be responsible for the purchase of one of those) out of the hat, I'd got him nothing so I felt adored, happy and really, *really* bad at the same time.

I have high hopes for this year.

I resolved to do what I could on a limited budget and even more limited energy. The Husband has always been a bit of a metrosexual at heart, though his nickname is Muscle Man because he did a bit of bodybuilding when we first met and could never wear a normal-sized shirt because of his massive neck – and arms, back, wrists, chest … Despite the cheesiness,

I know that a big box of chocolates and sickly card will still go down well. Although I can't match the high standards he set last year, I present his gift with a flourish and wait, preparing to blush at my romantic inventiveness.

'Umph … whaaa—' is his response when I lay his truffles on his bare chest as he wakes up.

'Your valentine, sweetheart,' I coo. It is quite tricky to maintain the turtle dove act as Boy Two has been chewing my bosoms off all night and the last thing I feel is flirty, but I think it best to have a go. Besides, he can't cash the cheques my body is writing as he has 40 minutes to get to work and it's hard to manage even a quickie when the clock radio sets off stirrings in Boy One's room across the hall.

'It's what? … It's today? … It's, um, thanks. Haven't got you anything, y'know,' he admits, sleepily.

Still thinking that somewhere may be a gift money can't buy, I bat those lashes still not glued together by sleep and reply: 'That's OK, darling, you've got all day.'

'Mm, I can't afford anything – we've just had a baby, you know.'

Really? I hadn't noticed.

'And I haven't got time to shop 'cos I'll be late home. The boss wants to go over the grants. I don't think we've got a hope in hell, but she wants us to try all the same. Probably won't be before 10 pm. That's OK, isn't it.' It isn't a question. On that note he stumbles off into the bathroom, scratching a buttock and leaving me with murder on my mind.

On top of this, the birth of his second son last month has still gone unmarked, though, to be fair, all he managed on the birth of the first were flowers from the supermarket and a Pot Noodle, so the bar was not set high. (That said, a Pot Noodle was the thing I most wanted in the world at that point, all sanity being out of the window as I was probably still high on pethidine.) This is the second time in as many months he's missed a Hallmark moment. Not that I'm keeping count... .

A bad day is made worse by having a trolley/car interface in Sainsbury's car park. Somewhat unfairly, the trolley wins. A large, angry gash appears down the passenger side of my car, denting both doors. The mental cash register rings up four figures with a 'Ding!'. It may only be a Fiat Multipla rather than an Audi, or a Porsche, but it is *my* Multipla. It is my 12-month-old Multipla and the only car I have ever bought from new. In places, if you can get beyond the trodden Hula Hoops and chocolate raisins, it still even has some new-car smell. And now it has a stupid, stupid hole in the side.

The Husband isn't best pleased but I blame him for it anyway. If he hadn't been working so late on grant applications and had been at home bathing and feeding the kids, I might have had a chance of some shut-eye and therefore wouldn't have been so spaced out as to prang the car. He retorts that surely I'd prefer he spent his time finding a full-time paying job rather than greasing Boy Two's creases with nappy cream. I have to admit, grudgingly, that he has a point. However it's still all his fault. On principle.

Friday 15 February 2008

When I was doing PR for a book I wrote a while back, I did the rounds of BBC local radio. This usually meant sitting in a little booth at Western House in central London, listening to a DJ in a far-off land via a pair of headphones and having a surreally pally conversation with the wall. One of the interviews, however, was with my local station, BBC Radio Berkshire, so it was just as easy to pop down the road and grace them with my presence. We had such a hoot that they invited me back again, and again, and again. What was a one-off puff for a book has now turned into a regular Friday slot doing the papers with Henry Kelly, the avuncular Irish broadcaster of Classic FM, *Game for a Laugh* and *Going for Gold* fame.

Though all of my stints are unpaid, I enjoy my weekly banter over the airwaves. Every now and again I entertain thoughts of sliding effortlessly into a job as a presenter but mostly I stick to the reality, which is that it's a bit of a laugh and handy if I ever need somewhere to plug anything. In fact, I don't fancy the thought of being replaced, which is why I go back less than a month after Boy Two's birth.

Throughout last year, my growing bump had been the sole topic of conversation on Henry's show. He delighted in telling me that 'boys make a disgrace of ye'. When I occasionally turned up on the Saturday show too, the DJ looked petrified that I'd pop on his studio floor while he was inadequately stocked with towels. Henry also kept threatening to send the radio car round to the Royal Berks maternity ward for a live outside broadcast of the happy event. I had to subtly inform him that of the emergency numbers pinned to the fridge, the outside broadcast unit at BBC Radio Berkshire was not one.

They probably think it's mad that a woman with a three-week-old baby is so keen to get back on air. But, now that I have some possible projects in the pipeline and there is still a rabid PR girl lurking inside, I'm damned if I'm going to let free airtime pass me by.

The bonus is that Henry's Producer Man is quite happy to look after Boy Two while I'm on air. Breastfeeding, burping and nappy changing aren't quite compatible with companionable banter on-air about the state of Reading Football Club's relegation prospects. I'm not at all worried about how Boy Two will react to a bosomless stranger for an hour or so, but how is poor old Producer Man to cope? Since the episode in the hairdresser's, Boy Two has been affectionately renamed 'the vomit comet'.

Sunday 17 February 2008

On a visit to worship at the chubby feet of Boy Two, Middle Sister suggests I get into child modelling. Well, not me, obviously, but the offspring. Once I've recovered from the laughing fit I have to concede that she has a point. My children aren't astoundingly beautiful by any stretch of the imagination. In fact, Boy Two's passport photo is back and in it he is doing a fine impression of a Hungarian shot-putter – male or female, take your pick. Now, naturally I think that the kids are stunning, but that's a mother's prerogative, along with believing that everyone else's children have appalling manners and are borderline ADHD.

However, Boy One certainly fits the wholesome, outdoorsy image favoured by kiddie catalogues – Boden and their ilk. Boy Two's bottom is just crying out for a Johnson's Baby Wipe to be artfully draped across it. Middle Sister says that a friend of her boyfriend's is a talent scout for this sort of thing and that she'll send over some pictures. It isn't really morally wrong to send a three-year-old out to work to support his parents' Merlot habit, is it?

After Middle Sister has left I crank up the internet and look into this modelling malarkey. Children don't have to be 'overly beautiful' (good), just 'clear-skinned and bright-eyed' (would chocolate-smeared with unidentifiable foodstuffs in the hair count?). They also have to be 'sociable, good at listening to instructions and carrying them out with the minimum of fuss'. This is all right for Boy Two who, having just discovered his smile, flirts with anything that moves, making for a very slow journey round the supermarket. Smiling babies are an absolute granny magnet.

Boy One, however, may prove a little trickier. Massively photogenic (like his mother, natch), he does have a tendency to try to crawl inside my clothes when he meets new people. It

doesn't take long for him to get over himself and start showing off like a pro, but probably long enough for ad men to get
bored and move on to the next angel-faced urchin. Equally:
'Bad manners or sulkiness will not be tolerated.' Boy One's
manners are fine but I'm a little sceptical about his Tourette-
like penchant for bellowing 'POO!' for no good reason. He
also does a nice line in teenage sulks if things aren't going his
way. (What will he do when he's a teenager – behave like a
toddler? It's not beyond the realms of imagination.)

Nor does it bode well that shoots can take 'two to three
hours, but factor in lots more time as they often overrun'.
Bored children, shyness followed by obstreperousness – it
doesn't sound like a recipe for an easy life. And then there is
the pay, which initially sounds great until you realise all the
'extras' you need to accommodate. Babies can coin in about
£50 an hour, and older children even more. But, and it's a
big 'but', the agencies take a quarter of that and you have to
be willing to leave everything at the drop of a hat, plus pay
for your own transport costs. Sure, one day they're grinning
over a bowl of peas and the next they're Patsy Kensit, married
to a rock star and doing a nice line in soap operas. But
twenty-odd years is a long time to wait to hit pay dirt. I've
given Middle Sister the go-ahead just in case something
comes of it, but I'm not sure that I'm suited to the role of
Mother of Supermodel.

Monday 18 February 2008

The good news is that the doula course stuff came through so I'm moments away from my new career as fanny monitor/urchin burper. However the bad news is that the course isn't until June, unless I want to attend the one in Manchester. It'd be fine for fitting into the grand scheme of using twelve months' maternity leave to set up an alternative to going back to the office, but leaving it that late doesn't cover me for the more immediate crisis posed by the Husband's lack of career prospects.

But, every cloud – silver lining and all that. Mr Book Man is champing at the bit for some more meat on the bones of this book idea we are tossing about. He reckons if he can get a full chapter breakdown, his editorial team will bite and we'll get the green light. I can't escape the irony that, after having decided writing isn't going to provide the bread and butter after having Boy Two, suddenly it's all taking off. I have even managed to use the delay in the doula course to pitch related stories to old freelance contacts. *The Times* blows me out as usual but my baby mag contacts seem really keen. I get roughly 350 smackers for every article I send them. It's not much but it keeps Boy One in Hula Hoops.

As I send off the chapter ideas to Mr Book Man, I reflect that I ought to get on with starting a business for myself, practising what I preach. But I still don't have a clue where to start. In a flagrant example of 'do as I say, not as I do', I've written in one of the sample chapters: 'You can always find time to squeeze in a phone call, meeting or web update – you just have to be creative! Use the crèche in the gym, the local playbarn or even beg a favour off a mate.' My latest business phone calls have been punctuated by hysterical screaming (Boy Two), chants of 'wipe my bottom, I did a poo' (Boy One), and several muffled moments as I dropped the phone that had been cradled between jaw and shoulder, both hands being occupied in wrestling a baby onto a boob.

Tuesday 19 February 2008

Finally, the Husband has finished his grant proposals. Instead of being swathed in a black cloud of despondency, he now carries an air of quiet resignation, born equally of not having much hope but being able to do bugger all about it. On the positive side this means he's a bit more available for bathing duty but it also means that his career – and our financial security – is in the hands of the gods, or charity accountants, which is practically the same thing.

Wednesday 20 February 2008

It seems I'm not the only one struggling with finding a new direction, post baby. Academic Mother brings her three-year-old daughter over for a playdate with Boy One and settles in for a good old whinge.

Shortly after having her daughter, Academic Mother resurrected her postgraduate thesis, aiming for a lectureship in one of the local universities. If I ever moaned about there not being enough hours in the day I just needed to look at her to get over myself. She rose at 4 or 5 am to start writing, getting her daughter up at 7 am and doing a full day of full-time parenting while her partner went out to work, putting her little girl to bed again at 8 pm only to pick up where she'd left off that morning. I don't think her head hit the pillow for more than three or four hours at any given time. She kept this up for nearly three years until she finally submitted her work, sailing through the viva and earning her PhD.

You'd have thought that it would have been the start of a glittering career... .

'The research just doesn't sit well with those conservative bastards,' she moans. 'I've got to get the thesis published and try to write a couple of really straight-laced articles before I'll fit in anywhere.'

'Weren't you helping out at some college or other?' I ask.

'Only one day a week, and it was only temporary. Besides, it didn't even keep the dog in balls.' Academic Mother's dog has a bit of a rubber fetish. 'I'm beginning to think there's no future in academia.' She sighs.

I could have told her that, based on the heavy depression hanging over our house at the moment.

'Your man won't be happy with you being a Stay at Home Mum surely. What are you going to do?'

Academic Mother's partner is certainly keen for her to get back to earning. He's an estate agent and the rocky economic climate isn't doing his employers any favours. His enthusiasm for her to start earning again doesn't extend to sharing the childcare though. I can't believe she hasn't folded under the sheer exhaustion of it all. The Husband may be many things, but he tries to be helpful and spends time with his children. I know I can count on his support, and for that I am always grateful.

'Ironically enough, I've gone into childcare – I'm registering as a childminder,' she answers. It makes sense, if you think about it. Apart from the enormous waste of lie-ins writing that bloody thesis, she's a natural mother and enjoys spending time with children. It's something I've thought about too, but only for a nanosecond because a) my house isn't big enough to swing a toddler – even a small one, and b) though I love my children deeply, the idea of singing 'Wind the Bobbin Up' for three hours straight makes me want to chew my own legs off.

Thursday 21 February 2008

I'm briefly leaving my country hovel to go and meet up with Mother from Work in London. She and I both work for the same magazine and have a peculiar habit of getting pregnant at the same time – twice so far. In fact, in our core team of four people there have been eight babies in the last four years. I think it's something to do with the chairs. We're both returning to what used to be the real world, a place where they get dressed before lunchtime. A place where they commute to offices and spend their time scanning Facebook for old boyfriends and sending emails to the person they sit beside.

We meet our Editrix in Starbucks and show off our respective babies. Mother from Work has already winkled out of me that I have no desire to go back. Nor has she, it seems. I won't say anything to the Editrix – I'm keeping my options open until the very last minute. It would be very embarrassing to have to eat my words and have to beg for my job back if it all goes pear-shaped for the Husband. I'm keeping everything crossed that it won't.

Having admitted to each other that neither intends going back, Mother from Work and I sit there feigning interest in the latest ad agency faux pas, or some consultancy that's showering the team with gifts and dreadfully purple PR prose for the magazine. I worked with some lovely people and we had great times but, as with all the best break-ups, it's not them, it's me. Oh, and the peanuts pay and the smelly bloke on the underground.

Tuesday 21 February 2008

One of the benefits of being on maternity leave is afternoon wine. I haven't been exploiting it fully until now because I am being a virtuous breastfeeding mother and trying to keep Boy Two off the Chianti for a few months at least. Also, I've just been too bloody busy to kick back with a glass or three.

My best friend from university in the east of Scotland somehow wound up living a mere five miles away in the deepest shires of England. Aside from the usual party nights and ill-advised snogs we have in common from our student days, we've also conspired to have babies only a few months apart. This provides endless scope for my Partner in Crime and I to gossip over a glass of wine and pick apart the horror that is OPC – other people's children.

Today, the Partner in Crime calls round with her little boy in one arm and a bottle of wine in the other. It will be rude not to join her in a glass or two.

After last week's trip to London, we get on to the topic of going back to work. I don't think I know anyone less enamoured of the idea of going back to work than Partner in Crime. But, because she feels that there really is no alternative, she's grasping the nettle and checking out nursery places, despite the fact that her son isn't even six months old. Loathe as she is to leave him, if she has to then she's going to make damn sure that she leaves him in the best place possible. And now it seems as though the good ones got snapped up moments after she left the delivery suite. She likes what she sees well enough, but she's only just getting used to mornings of Kindermusic and trips to the park rather than to the water cooler. I think for her to feel happy about leaving her son with someone else, they have to be one step away from sainthood.

To be honest, Partner in Crime is unlikely to really need to work anyway. Her husband has a good job and they live in a fourteenth-century, original-features-intact house with a teeny mortgage in the centre of one of south Oxfordshire's most genteel market towns. It was recently voted as having the most expensive real estate anywhere in the UK. Of course, things can go wrong, the value of shares, houses and marriages can go down as well as up, but the chances in her case are slim. But while part of her is just blissed out spending every waking moment with her baby, there's still another side of her that can't quite let go of the university-educated, emancipated career woman thing.

As we mull over our options I tell her about the doula thing I'm planning and explain that it's all about being a mother's help as well as a labour partner. She opines that she could do with one of those just on a day-to-day basis. Unlike me she doesn't have any regular childcare so planning a lunch or going to appointments means relying on the in-laws or baby comes too. What she could really do with, she says, is a babysitter on call.

'You can always call me,' I suggest. 'I couldn't be a child-minder full-time, but I don't mind a spot of child-wrangling now and then. Especially if there's a bottle of wine in it for me.'

'Thanks, but wouldn't it be nice if we didn't have to rely on hugger-mugger help from friends? I feel like I'm imposing ...' she says, worried.

'Not at all, I'd help where I could,' I reply, and I would, except I have to admit that I barely have time to look after my own children, let alone someone else's at the moment. I have a deadline for a thrilling article on breastfeeding and I still don't have any answers for my mumpreneur dilemma.

But then I have what can only be described as a Eureka moment, without the overflowing bath and wrinkly Greek man, obviously. If we both needed someone to sort things out for us, take care of babysitting, wait in for deliveries and so on, then there must be plenty of women in the same boat. What if we get together some mums looking to earn cash, who we could send out in times of need? We'd be the Ticketmaster of babysitting, a concierge service for harassed mums, a mumciergery!

Becoming excited at the prospect of not having to go back to work gets the Partner in Crime's creative juices flowing and soon we're talking about party organising, managing mums' diaries and all sorts of services. Fuelled by wine we get a bit excited and start sorting out all the important details – who is going to appear on *GMTV*, what wardrobe suits the joint CEOs of a booming mumcierge business, whether a trip to Selfridges to acquire said wardrobe is a bit premature, which exotic island we can retreat to on holiday to spend the profits.

I call the Husband full of excitement that we are on the way with a proper business idea, one that will make money and have employees and be famous and everything. He puts on his best 'indulging the little wife' voice and asks, 'How exactly is this going to make money, and who will be looking after our children while you're building this empire?'

I'm on too much of a high, and possibly a little drunk, to care that he isn't exactly bowled over by our magical money-making schemes. In fact, in my mind we're practically in profit already.

Wednesday 27 February 2008

I'm still basking in the glow of my new-found mumpreneur status. At last I feel as though there is actually a business from which I can make some real money. I spend the day research-ing the competition, and find there isn't any – well, there is an identical service in west London, but as that is over 40 miles away and this kind of thing is a bit dependent on help being practically round the corner, I don't think we need to worry about them. It does mean that we can pinch, or rather be inspired by, the things they have already set up. Bonus! I've been trying to come up with a mission statement for our new mumciergery as well. We also need a decent brand name because mumciergery is, frankly, a bit weird.

I take a break from empire-building to go and collect Boy One from pre-school. His teacher greets me with what I take to be an admiring look as I troop up with the baby in a sling. 'That baby is still practically a newborn,' I imagine her think-ing, 'and here she is already back in the groove. What an inspiration!' Perhaps I just exude success... .

Walking home reflecting on her obvious admiration, I can't resist a quick preen in a nearby shop window. Quick flick of the hair, and I'm a picture of yummy mumminess framed in the dark glass, with Boy One frolicking beside me and Boy Two angelically asleep tucked against my side. That and the two dinner-plate-sized orbs of leaking milk darkening my top. What I had taken for admiration was obviously indulgent pity as she thought to herself, 'Bless her, she's so sleep-deprived and hormone-addled that she hasn't noticed her milk's come in again. Maybe the poor love's in such a state she's plain forgotten to feed the baby.' Not Superwoman, then. Bugger.

Sunday 2 March 2008

Mother's Day. I remember the Husband talking about Mother's Day shortly after the birth of Boy One. In obvious shock at someone having driven a bus through his wife's lady-parts, he said to the midwife: 'Now I understand what the fuss is all about. I'm never going to give my mother a crap present again. And I'd better make sure our son looks after his mum too!' Three years and one more son and heir down the line and what do I get for this special day? Nada, nothing, zip. So that's the birth in January, Valentine's Day in February and Mother's Day in March – three months, three Hallmark moments missed and I'm not impressed.

I'm only slightly mollified by the fact that my old book's

biggest selling season is just before Mother's Day so it should have been flying off the shelves as desperate dads and children snap up anything with 'mum' in the title to dispense their duties for another year. Our skiing holiday is imminent so it's comforting to think that the vins chauds and après ski aperitifs are being taken care of.

Friday 7 March 2008

Finally the long-awaited skiing holiday rolls around. But it also reminds me how little time has actually passed. Barely six weeks ago we were rushing out of the delivery suite to post Boy Two's passport application. In the interim I've found two new careers and discovered that I can – almost – function on three hours' sleep in every twenty-four. Things look rosy. Even the prospect of spending ten hours taking five separate trains across Europe with two small children can't dampen my spirits.

Of course, the Husband's precarious work situation is overshadowing things a little. Both the doula and mumcierge ideas could bring in a decent part-time income but on their own they won't be enough to sustain our growing (grown? I'm really not in the market for a third) family if his (the main) breadwinning income is taken away. There's still a very real possibility that I'm going to be back at my desk in less than three months. But now is not the time to think of such things. Instead it's time to think of cutting through fresh powder and ignoring the fashionistas' advice to slap on the sunblock. Even if it stops at a tide mark round my neck, I'm determined to get a tan.

Sunday 9 March 2008

First day of the holiday and instead of trooping straight up the hill, the Husband has curled up in an armchair, resembling a deflated Michelin man in his salopettes. He's trying to steal Wi-Fi. It seems we can't live without a permanent umbilical cord to the outside world. Miraculously he finds one. Webmail should, must, be read. And it cheers up my non-skiing father-in-law no end to discover that he can get the boxing results as a reward for being tied to fibreglass and thrown off the top of a rock, then left to hurtle down a sheet of ice with only a small, spiky forest to use as brakes.

Wednesday 12 March 2008

So far on my relaxing holiday I have:

- Cooked five dinners for six people.
- Used the medieval torture device known as a breast pump to extract two feeds a day for the baby, to be delivered into his gaping maw by my mother-in-law while I'm up a mountain.
- Answered twelve emails covering, variously, names for

the mumciergery, the impossibility of getting a criminal records bureau check and the consequent absolute necessity of one, queries regarding the potty training article (apparently, in one of the case studies where a boy had learned to do a poo in the big toilet, I'd put his age at 33. They wanted to check this is what I meant. I mean, it wouldn't occur to them that the extra '3' was a typo or anything).

- Fallen over three times – twice when Boy One snow-ploughed into me at speed, having learned how to start, but not how to stop. The third was when the Husband also used my ankles as a braking device, scything into my legs with his skis and rearranging my kneecaps.

- That I have had only one hour-long crying fit after all this is, I think, a good thing.

Monday 17 March 2008

We survived yesterday's epic journey home from the Alps despite Boy One's constant diarrhoea on the Eurostar. Fortunately he is still in night nappies so we had something to catch the accidents, but inevitably the nappy supply ran out somewhere under the Channel. We resorted to padding out his underpants with bits of newborn nappy that we hoped Boy Two would not require before we reached home.

Our happiness at being back home is short-lived, not least because of the three separate credit card bills waiting for

me on the welcome mat. I always feel the worst bit about
going on holiday is not knowing what you'll come back to. I
fantasise about break-ins, fires, floods and unpayable bills
languishing on the mat. On this occasion we avoid all but the
last. As I hide the offending articles from the Husband I pray
to the god of re-mortgaging, hoping that our recent switch
between banks will see much-needed funds land in our
account soon.

At least I don't need to worry about a slew of demanding
emails because I've pretty much kept up with them while
we've been away. Some might say you're wrecking your holiday by never leaving work alone, but I say that I'd wreck it
anyway by worrying about what was going on in my absence.

What I didn't bank on was other people holding on to
their bad news emails until I got back. While we've been away,
someone has published a 'How to' book on becoming a
mumpreneur that is almost identical to the one I have in the
pipeline. No funny business, just a coincidence that someone
else had the same cracking idea, but about four months
earlier. Mr Book Man drops the proposal like a hot rock. As
I've mentally already spent the advance and, reading the credit
card statements, have actually spent some of it too, this is a bit
of a blow. Never mind, there are still the proceeds of the
mother's day book, the latest payment instalment for which is
due any day now.

Friday 21 March 2008

Galvanised into action by the sudden vacuum in the family finances I kick the Husband out of the house on Good Friday to fetch chocolate eggs and distract the children while I get on with some work. I still need brand names – mum4hire? Mumsitters? – and a website, posters, fliers …

This leads me to making yet more to-do lists with action points and division of tasks between my Partner in Crime and me, involving neatly folded paper and different coloured pens. I have always had this fetish: I have written the list, ergo the job has been done. Which of course it hasn't and I've spent so long cataloguing jobs to do I no longer have any time left to do them. The Husband is now back with the children – one of them is high on chocolate and the other is desperate for some boob. Project millionaire is postponed for another day.

Saturday 22 March 2008

At last the unmistakable franked envelope from my first ever publisher plops heavily through the letter box. I'm not ashamed to say I practically drop the baby on the floor in the rush for it. Figures baffle me at the best of times but I'm fairly sure that the number of minus signs next to four- and five-figure numbers is not encouraging. Matched by the virtual tumbleweed blowing through my online banking account I think it's safe to say that those minus signs mean what I think they do. To cheer myself up, I hop in the car to go to the supermarket. I intend to spend next month's freelance income (not actually commissioned but hey, it's on the list) on baby trinkets and wine.

Or that is the intention but I am in such a hurry that I prang my neighbour's car while executing a speedy three-point turn. He is parked on the double yellows that are there precisely to give you enough space to do a three-point turn without hitting any parked cars. I call the insurance company and pretend to be on their side:

'I hit his driver-side bumper but it's only a wee scratch really.'

'So it's your fault, madam?'

'Ye-es, but he's parked on the double yellows that are there to let you turn safely. Really, it's his fault because he shouldn't have parked there in the first place. If it's his fault then you should refuse to pay. That I get to keep my No Claims is neither here nor there.'

'But, madam, you were moving, he was not. Therefore, it's your fault, your claim, your insurance and your No Claims, I'm afraid. I'd say you were into him by about £500.'

'Bugger.'

It's not 1 April yet, is it?

Chapter 3

Sleepless Nights

Thursday 3 April 2008

You know that you're a proper mumpreneur when you find yourself fixing your make-up in the dark in an underground car park using little more than Touche Éclat and a pair of blue Noddy pants, age 2–3.

I'm venturing out into the big wide world today. Often there aren't just days but weeks when I don't go much further than the edge of the village. But today I'm going up to town, to the smoke, to London. I've arranged to meet an old contact from my PR days who knows a bit about start-up businesses and how to go about getting them going.

The thrill of being allowed back into the world of the grown-ups (mothers' corner at playgroup doesn't count) is swiftly extinguished by yet another wardrobe crisis. That joey pouch is refusing to budge despite me spending the last four weeks pounding on the treadmill. Bosoms are also an issue, insofar as they don't stay inside anything that's not made of metres of cotton jersey. Shirts are a definite no-no as my cleavage is paying tribute to *Debbie Does Dallas*. I eventually drag on a dress which somehow manages to be both frumpy (hemline) and whoreish (neckline) at the same time. Hopefully the Pepto-Bismol-hued pashmina will distract my friend's attention.

At least this time I remember the breast pads. Three weeks ago I was happily burbling away at Henry K on the radio show when I felt the telltale tingle under my armpits. This signals that I have exactly thirty seconds to deploy padding before the milk dam bursts and my top starts to darken in two very unmistakable ways. Halfway through dissecting the American Presidential Primaries I nonchalantly crossed my arms, hoping no one noticed me trying to stem the tide. I'm sure Henry thought it slightly odd that I kissed him goodbye and tried to leave the studio at the end of the show still with my arms firmly crossed over my chest.

My meeting today is instructive:

- Could I cope if lots of mums wanted to use the service straight away? (Probably, maybe, in fact no, not really.)
- Could I survive financially if no one used it straight away? (See 1.)
- Had I thought about marketing, had I developed a distinct brand and did I have a budget set aside for it? (Yes, no and although I have a percentage of revenues set aside for marketing, 10 per cent of nothing is still nothing so, no.)

- Was there a distinct division of labour between Partner in Crime and me to establish roles, boundaries, remuneration, etc. (No, in fact I haven't seen her in ages. Must do something about that.)
- Had I arranged my tax, insurance, qualifications, criminal record checks, etc.? (No, no, no and um, no. Oh dear.)

There's a saying: 'If you're not part of the solution, you're part of the problem.' Well, there are precious few solutions that come out of my meeting but a massive list of problems. At least I had a fairly comprehensive to-do list. I suppose I should be depressed that I thought I was good to go and it seems that I'm not even 5 per cent of the way to getting going on my own. But strangely I'm not. Now I've got my list of things to get on with, and if they're all completed satisfactorily, I should have me a business.

Saturday 5 April 2008

Boy One has a date at his friend's birthday party. Twenty screaming children aged three and four rampaging round a playbarn fuelled by cheesy puffs, cake and lemonade. This doesn't frighten me as much as perhaps it should because:

- it's someone else's party,
- in someone else's building, and
- in two hours Boy One will experience a massive sugar

crash and lie comatose and drooling in front of *The Lion King* until it's time for an early bed.

Therefore I can look forward to a longish period of peace and quiet this evening. I think I may sleep. Haven't done that for a while.

Sunday 1 April 2008

Party was a great success except Boy One is now determined to have his own bash there in September. This will, I fear, be expensive and painful. However it has made me realise something about starting up this concierge service. Managing people doesn't bother me, the tax situation is baffling but I'm sure I'll figure it out. Setting up websites and whatnot is actually quite fun (new career as an IT wonk? Not impossible). But, by offering a party helper service as part of our package, it dawns on me that I could be stuck in a kids' party filled with hyperactive three-year-olds every Saturday from now until the hereafter. This is terrifying.

I also give Boy One his biannual haircut today. I usually wait until 40-year-olds start saying, 'What a pretty girl!' before deciding he needs a trim. We're going for the long-locked surfer dude look at the moment. The haircutting experience usually consists of a large bar of chocolate to keep him still, large quantities of spray-on conditioner to get the dreadlocks out and the kitchen scissors.

So far I've entertained the idea of starting up as a PR, childminder, doula, radio presenter and website manager. I don't think we'll be adding hairdresser to that list.

Wednesday 9 April 2008

We make yet another pilgrimage to the venerated grandmother north of the border. It's nice to visit the old home town. In a life where I've picked up two fathers, four mothers, two half-siblings and three step-siblings, seven schools and twelve family homes – and that's just up to age 16 – it's nice to know that Gma and Gpa stayed put in the same village for all of my nearly 35 years. Gpa's moved on to stay with some floozies with white dresses and wings and a big bloke with a beard, but Gma's feet are still firmly planted on Scottish soil (as opposed to in it).

Indeed, there is much to love about the old family homestead: discovering an old printing kit I was given for Christmas 1983, ink all dried up and letters missing; or finding the electronic keyboard Gpa made for me out of wood, a sheet of aluminium, some wires and a battery bigger than his fist. The benefit of having a relative with a double first in Physics and Maths and part of the team that developed RADAR was that he could take a bundle of wires, wood and metal and make something really quite wonderful. You can take your Barbie, I'll have my home-made stylophone any day.

Unfortunately, despite being fascinated by computers and

the internet, my Gpa selfishly failed to install broadband into the bungalow before he popped off to electrify the angels' harps. So here I am armed with a laptop and a feature on toddler play to file by tomorrow and no way of getting on the internet, not even with dial-up.

We are but minutes from Silicon Glen where many of the IT advances were made in the 1980s and 1990s but I can't get a signal on my mobile or connect to the internet. With my web habit this is a serious problem. Nor does Gma's village have anything like an internet café. It has a café but the only cookies they're interested in have chocolate chips and go nicely with a cuppa.

In the end I resort to filing copy the way so many hacks did before the war – over the phone, using my voice instead of the beeeee-awwwww-bipbip-beeeennnnnnggg of the modem.

I'm also too embarrassed to do this direct to the editor of the magazine. After all why pay a freelancer to dictate to you something that you may just as well have knocked up yourself? Instead I call Middle Sister who is handily at her desk in a super-cool sports and music marketing agency in London.

I wonder what they make of:

'"Your toddler will enjoy shouting rude words like POO and WILLY" – got that?'

'Do you want me to capitalise all of poo and willy?'

'Yes, please.'

I hope her boss in their nice open plan office is understanding.

Tuesday 15 April 2008

The trip to Scotland was nice but it puts us all out of sorts. Perhaps it's the seven-hour slog up and down the M1 in the middle of the night that does it. You can't contemplate a journey like that during the day. Bored children with permanently full bladders make for slow progress. And during the brief moments when you are actually making time up the motorway the children are bouncing up and down in the back, hyped on sugar from the endless chocolate bribery. Boy Two is a little young for the sugar rush but Boy One has a surprisingly long reach for someone strapped into a car seat.

So an overnight drive it is, speeding through the wee hours down the coast, listening to mad programmes on Radio 2. The Husband ponders why stations insist on playing bagpipe music or Wagner when you really need a bit of Bon Jovi or The Eagles to keep you going. But the children are both snoring peacefully in the back so we have to be grateful for small mercies.

At one point we both get hit by a dose of the snoozes so we need something more peppy to keep us going. The Husband has stored some comedy on his MP3 player so we plug in a bit of Billy Connolly to blow the cobwebs away. We're right in the middle of a lovely juicy skit about inventive sex, in which Billy C gets himself in a right old froth and shouts, 'FUUUUCCK, Fucking FUUUUCK!' with great gusto, when a little voice from the back pipes up:

'He said "fucking", Mummy. Has he got naughty manners?'

I find myself completely incapable of speech. I'm trying so hard to stop myself from laughing that I clamp my mouth shut and my eyes well up. The pressure threatens to blow my ears off. It's just as well there are few other cars about because I'm finding it hard to see. Eventually the Husband recovers his composure long enough to say:

'Very naughty manners, darling. Now, how about a bit of "Puff the Magic Dragon"?'

The humorous interlude is unfortunately short-lived. Every time we do this trip the combination of petrol station food, recycled air and sleep deprivation leaves us all twitchy and tetchy. Back home the Husband starts to pick on the state of the house, a niggle that then swiftly descends into the usual argument over money or, more importantly, the lack of it:

'I just can't stand all this clutter, it makes me claustrophobic,' he complains.

'It's only Boy Two's toys and he'll grow out of these soon, then we can get rid of them.'

'But can't you put them somewhere?'

'We don't really have anywhere to put them, but I have ordered some storage boxes to go under Boy One's bed. When they arrive we could stuff a lot in them.'

'How much did they cost?'

'About £80. Why?'

'You shouldn't be spending any money. We don't even know if I'm going to have a job in a month. You don't seem to have got anywhere with this business thing.'

'It takes time to get going.'

'You haven't even got a name yet.'

'The name's the most important thing, I've got to get that right. And what about you? We'd have had that cheaper mortgage if you'd got your paperwork to me in time.'

With that I deal the decisive blow. The Husband is on my case in a second if I let a credit card bill go past the payment date. He is an arch-interest avoider. And yet when we had to bail from our mortgage company last month because the monthly payment went stratospheric, he dithered for so long about getting his proof of salary to the new one that we lost the low percentage deal. I managed to secure another one that was only a tiny bit more expensive but not before blubbing down the phone to the operator. She must have thought I was a victim of spousal abuse:

'It's just [*sob*] that my husband won't help me.'

'I'm sorry, we can't get that rate back. The system's automated.'

'But we had everything, all the papers but his and he wouldn't pull his finger out [*sob*]. Can't you do *anything*?'

'Sorry.'

The new deal we finally secured wasn't a great deal more expensive than the first but I now have some great ammunition to shut the Husband up when he starts nagging. I'm not sure how long I can get away with it for, though.

Thursday 17 April 2008

Returning from the shops I find a waif and stray on my doorstep. I often find friends and acquaintances loitering on my doorstep as it's a conveniently warm place to hide if you miss your train, what with the station being barely a two-minute walk away. Anecdotally, ours seems to be the coldest station in England with an icy wind howling past the platforms as frequently as the trains. Of course, being of good Scots stock and naturally well-insulated, I don't find this a problem at all. I am, however, surrounded by soft, southern Sassenachs.

Perched on kerb is in fact the Partner in Crime's husband, the Family Friendly Businessman. Though he's often away for days at a time on business, when he is home he's a real hands-on dad and you can tell from his expression that he genuinely loves kids. Mind you, he's quite slender so he clearly couldn't eat a whole one.

I invite him in for a coffee and small talk while we wait for the telltale horn sounding at the bottom of the garden that tells him his next train has arrived. He reveals that he and the Partner in Crime have been discussing this mumciergery idea already. As it will affect his family finances as well as mine, and therefore he has a pretty big say in whether or not she goes ahead with it, I tentatively ask him if he thinks it's a goer, really not wanting to hear the wrong answer.

But Family Friendly Businessman thinks that a mumciergery should fly with no problem. But …

And then he spends the next half-hour coming up with all sorts of questions that I have no idea how to answer. It shows how little I'd thought this through. If I charge a booking fee but I'm not there to enforce it, what's to stop people bypassing me and going straight to the source? Have I got a criminal record check and do I realise how hard it is to get one? What about insurance – what would happen if a child choked while in my care? Could I cope with offering all these services at once – shouldn't I think about starting out smaller?

I try to keep smiling in the face of this onslaught but in my head all I can think is 'What the hell have I let myself in for?' Finally, the horn sounds and Family Friendly Businessman shoots out through the door to catch his train. I'm left with a head swarming with more questions than answers. To shut them out I self-medicate with a large glass of wine and crappy telly. Am I going to have to rethink the whole thing?

Monday 21 April 2008

Out of the blue a child modelling agency gets in touch about the email I sent them weeks ago. They're interested in getting Boy One on their books and would I mind bringing him for an 'audition'. This sounds like a sensible option while I wait to get everything else off the ground, until I read further.

Would I also mind paying a couple of hundred quid for his portfolio shots, oh, and his insurance premium. Plus, they can't really guarantee he would be used in the campaign shots that they have in mind for him as the client will 'order' a few boys to come along and only use the one that looks best on camera. Apparently you'll get paid a nominal fee for them to go along, but only the boy who is to be used in the campaign will get his hands on the moolah.

Due to the ongoing failure of the new mortgage company to provide us with the actual mortgage, money is getting a little tight. I got away with insisting to the Husband that we spend a few hundred pounds teaching me how to deal with screaming women but I don't think he's going to be happy about funding the next Naomi Campbell (I can't think of any well-known male 'Naomis' – perhaps that should tell me something about Boy One's potential career trajectory as a model?). I send the agency a polite thanks but no thanks on this occasion, making up a spurious story about getting over a bug and not being in the most cooperative mood. I initially wondered about pretending that he had chicken pox but thought better of it as they'd instantly think 'spotty, scarred' and therefore modelling career aborted before it began. Perhaps with a bit more money in the kitty in the next few weeks I'll call them back to get that portfolio done, but not right now. We need to eat.

And despite the flow of funds dwindling to a trickle, we are eating rather well. I am in love with Ocado. As I'm perpetually tied to the computer anyway, I decide to shop online instead of schlepping to the supermarket every day. I'm going to try to train myself to do the weekly shop, rather than the daily impulse buy. And, apart from the fact that I'm wedded to posh shopping, I love that they'll deliver for free at 10 pm after the kids are in bed. The Husband is mollified by the fact that they claim to be no more expensive than Tesco and Boy One thinks Santa comes every week now. If he's refusing to go to bed I say, 'You have to be asleep when the man with the van comes or he'll realise you're awake and won't leave any treaties for the treaty basket.' Oh Mr Sandman, bring me some bream, and the sweetest taters, that I've ever seen... .

Tuesday 22 April 2008

I get my first taste of what it will be like to run the mumcierge service. One of Boy One's friends came over to be child-minded today. The Very Capable Childminder had to go to an appointment so I took her only other ward. Normally with a house full of three-year-olds, I'd let them tear around the house and garden, refereeing fights from a distance, lazily blowing kisses from the sofa to kiss anything better and surveying the damage long after everyone has gone home. However, because I'm 'on' in a professional capacity, I feel I have to loiter no more than 5 feet from their every position.

This means marshalling games of 'bonk each other on the head with a tennis racket', 'lob the ball into next door's garden' and 'running in circles really fast until you fall over in the funniest way possible'. For its novelty value it's amusing but each game rapidly becomes crashingly boring. The Very Capable Childminder earns her money twelvefold. Just don't tell her that or she'll put her rates up.

Sunday 27 April 2008

From tomorrow, Boy One will be at pre-school in the afternoons as well as the mornings. It's going to be bliss. This means I will be able to achieve more than simply the journey to and from the school, one supermarket shop and one nappy change before the three-year-old whirlwind returns. I might even be able to – gulp – get some work done. If only Boy Two would sleep! Goodness knows I can. Aren't babies supposed to be sleeping for around 16 hours in 24 at this point. Now, I know that I'm not getting that much sleep, so why won't he stick to what the book says? Honestly, can't he read!

Monday 28 April 2008

I got back from an interview at 9.45 am and am already so tired I don't know what to do with the day. *BBC Breakfast* rather deliciously wanted me on at 7ish to talk about the insanity that is Nannycams – plastic trinkets that 'hide' a camera where you can check up on the hired help. I have never seen anything that so obviously screams WE'RE WATCHING YOU! If you're so scared about leaving your children alone, don't. And if you have to, do your research, don't just abandon them with the local psycho and hope for the best, secure in the knowledge that if they're being slapped six ways from Saturday, you can watch it all happen 40 miles and two hours away.

Despite a background as a cynical hackette, I still get excited about the prospect of being on the goggle box (if TV is a goggle box, does that make a computer the google box?). The first time I was on TV it was about men being useless at home. I suggested on air that they weren't and that division of labour was key. However, as my maths isn't up to squat, division of labour at our house comes down to: work divided by 2 = emptying dishwasher by husband + rest of everything by me.

And I suspect the first time I was on I couldn't have been too coherent, since I was horrifically hungover. When I got the call the night before (being called onto *BBC Breakfast* is all very urgent, last-minute stuff and is a deeply thrilling 'I only got the call at 6 pm the night before and simply didn't have a thing to wear' affair), I got all overexcited and insisted on bending the Husband's ear about how great I was going to be over several gins and bottles of white. As I was being conveyed in a luscious Jag – nice to see the wise use of my licence fee, Auntie, by the way – to Broadcasting House at 5 am the following day, or it could have been the same night for that matter, I was clutching my 2-litre bottle of water very tightly and attempting to turn my eyeballs from pink back to white. The make-up ladies were very sympathetic and didn't mention the fact that I was sweating pure ethanol. And apparently studio lights are so strong they bleach out your eyes anyway, hence the orange pancake make-up.

This time I didn't make the mistake of staying up all night drinking. Instead I stayed up all night breastfeeding. The pink eyes were still there and instead of ethanol I seemed to be sweating Gold Top. What poor Sian Williams thinks of me I do not know.

But even with an hour's sleep and leaking boobs, I'm ducking and diving, doing deals. Once I was back in the green room (an affront to trades descriptions since it is the orange broom cupboard), I had a chance to chat with the bloke I was pontificating on screen with. He's the publisher of a dads' mag and I'm anxious to get my foot in the door. Much as I'm getting excited by my nascent mumciergery, wonga for words is what's currently paying the bills and it's good to have a standby. I loosely pitch a couple of ideas at him and leave it at that.

Tuesday 29 April 2008

Call the editor of the dads' mag to go over what I'd said to his publisher yesterday morning, but he's not in so I leave a message. On the school run I bump into the Glamazon. She's a fellow pre-school mum and I'm always guaranteed to bump into her when I've failed to shower for three days and have dragged something to wear out of the washing up box. Never leaving the house without full warpaint, she's got this old school glamour thing going on. Masses of long, wavy black hair, eyes kohl'd to the max, red lips and HUGE Jackie O sunglasses, she positively sashays. She's also filled with boundless energy and seems to know everyone in the village as the playground echoes to 'DARLING!! How ARE you?!' at 3pm every day. She's a blast.

We get talking about deadlines as you do and she mentions that she's running late on one for this men's magazine she occasionally writes for, one for the dads. I realise that this must be the same magazine I was talking about with *BBC Brekkie* and get all excited that we have a shared interest.

The second thought I have, following hot on the heels of the first is 'Oh bugger – I've just tried to poach this woman's column from under her.' The editor must realise that we've got the same dialling code and, as we're in the sticks, we must live very close to each other. I hope he doesn't call her to tell her. Hacks can be at each other's throats for the exclusive on a story, but equally it's bad form to poach a column from under a fellow hackette's feet. Particularly when you share the school run. Frantically think of ways to get her onside – perhaps she'd like to be in the mumcierge biz?

Chapter 4

Teething Troubles

Monday 5 May 2008

Realising that the possibility of getting the mumciergery off the ground any time soon is unlikely, and having to wait until next month for the doula training course, I need to get money coming in somehow. My only real recourse is to go back to hawking stories round publishers again.

I may as well write about what I know so I send several beautifully crafted story breakdowns about becoming a doula and trying to set up a business as a Stay At Home Mum. Convinced that these are the topics *du jour* I can't help but imagine that the commissions will come rolling in. I email the Husband to warn him that he may be needed for babysitting cover in the next few days as I'll be busy churning out copy for magazines and newspapers – I'm convinced that the Saturday *Times* will snap up the doula story, Labour's failure to provide adequate maternity care being one of their favourite drums to beat.

Tuesday 1 May 2008

Nothing. Not a sausage. *The Times* replies to say they did a story on doulas two years ago and therefore it was recent history. The parenting magazines don't bother replying. A follow-up call to one reveals they haven't even looked at it as their commissioning editor is on maternity leave and they seem less than keen to fill her shoes, claiming: 'We have enough stories for the time being.'

I would say I'll go on to plan B but I don't really have one. Should I just calm down a bit, wait for the doula course and stick with that? What about the mumciergery? It seems like such a good idea; there must be a market for it. The Partner in Crime and I will both be gutted if we decide to give it a miss then some bored, filthy rich housewife decides to give it a go and makes an absolute fortune, cornering the market in our area completely.

I don't have to make a decision about anything this very instant. I'm lucky that I'm getting payment of sorts for maternity leave, not that it leaves you enough for shopping anyway. It's a treat not to buy own-brand pasta at the moment. Still, it would be nice to have some kind of income to fatten up the bank balance. Plus, the novelty of sitting around watching daytime TV has worn off a bit. Yes, it's great that I now see a lot more of Boy One and Boy Two is getting some quality parenting. I'm even seeing more of the Husband although in his current state of mind it's debatable as to whether or not this is a good thing. I'm in danger of getting bored and over-drawn so clearly I should be doing something…

But, that said, is it really worth getting stressed out by my baby's cries because I *just* need to send this email, or really should go to this business seminar. Not as placid as his brother was as a baby, Boy Two commands the attention of everyone in the room. Though I'm much better at ignoring his cries when I need to (when you gotta pee, you gotta pee), nevertheless I feel very neglectful when my child howls for Mummy's attention and I'm doing nothing more important than fiddling with Google adwords.

I'm so confused about which path I should be following that I'm tempted to chuck it all in here and now. After all, I have a three-month-old baby and a further nine months of maternity leave to look forward to. What's the rush?

Oh, the thud of the credit card bills on the mat and the 'insufficient funds' message flashing at me from the cash point. That would be the rush, then.

Wednesday 7 May 2008

I am officially permitted by the Husband to shop online, as long as it's eBay and as long as I've sold something first. You have to give them their due, PayPal and eBay make a really sensible partnership. You sell something through eBay and they put the proceeds in an account which eventually decants into a nominated account after a period of a couple of months.

However, if you make a purchase via PayPal before that happens, then they just take the money out of your account again. It's like having free cash!

The Husband therefore thinks this is a good idea and condones my shopping habit as long as it doesn't come out of his gold card account: (He thinks my meagre maternity pay is taking care of essential bills and grocery shopping right now. What he doesn't know is that his gold card details are safely saved in our – i.e. my – Ocado account and I regularly siphon off a hundred quid's worth of grocery shopping each week.)

Today I am awaiting the result of one particular bid with feverish excitement. Since he was born, Boy Two has refused to sleep anywhere but underneath my armpit. Oh, early on he tried to kid us with his super-hero napping powers but that soon changed. Now the tiniest sound rouses him from his slumber and puts a big dent in my plans for the day.

It's the same only worse at night, when he is most keen on snacking at all hours, every single one of them if possible. I frequently find myself dozing off at 2 am, and wake again at 2.30 to find him still lazily chomping away. Every attempt to relocate him to his cot seems to go well but no sooner have I gently slid into the arms of the Husband than a piercing shriek demands that I return immediately to the scene of his abandonment and return him to the breast.

This palaver has me right at the end of my tether and despite protestations that I would never buy any more major pieces of baby equipment after the birth of the second child,

I just have to find a drop bedside cot from somewhere. They somehow manage to stay upright with only three sides in tact, because the mattress butts right up against the double bed, allowing mum to slide a sleeping baby gently off the tit and across into their own bed.

Only one hitch, on our limited budget of around zero pounds: with bedside cots costing little shy of three hundred pounds, I can see the Husband swallowing this one even less easily than the modelling idea.

But, as usual, eBay is my friend and there looks to be a pick-up-only job (usually a lot cheaper as only people nearby dare bid) going for the relative steal of £80. Of course, I'll have to spend a small fortune on diesel to get to … Guildford, but if it guarantees me more than 30 minutes of continuous sleep I'd drive to Calais if need be – without the help of a ferry.

Monday 12 May 2008

The Partner in Crime and I meet to try to make more arrangements for the mumcierge service. On the agenda today is the need to sort out the name, the basic offering, a timetable of work and a task list to divvy up the jobs.

Naturally, we spend the time drinking wine, catching her crawling baby before he does forward rolls down the stairs, and gossiping about others' poor parenting skills. We achieve absolutely nothing.

Thursday 15 May 2008

I have an appointment for some extreme beautifying. So far my anti-wrinkle regime has been based on a regular application of chocolate, on the basis that 'fat doesn't crack'. However it does seem to get riven with broken veins. I've always put up with what is commonly termed a ruddy complexion but lately I blush not just red but puce, and alcohol turns me into a heat lamp. Sleepless nights and crying babies notwithstanding, it's also really ageing.

As I need to get off my backside and take a more proactive, face-to-face approach to publicising the mumcierge business, the sight of an aged, exhausted mother is not going to inspire confidence. I head off to a posh private clinic to see a woman about a laser. The self-confidence isn't helped by much nodding and umming, which she follows with the assertion:

'We'll probably need the strong laser.'

Unfortunately she also notes that I won't be able to have the treatment until I stop breastfeeding Boy Two. This won't happen in the near future, not because I'm a hemp-wearing earth mother, but because our precarious financial situation, exacerbated by the Husband's career no-man's-land, is making me super tight with money. I refuse to shell out for milk if I can make it for free. I'm already looking for secret ways to break into our local allotment. And I realise that spending two hundred smackers on having bits of my face burned off is hardly the corner stone of a frugal existence, however I view it as a business expense. Window-dressing, if you like.

The appointment goes on longer than I anticipated and I find myself tearing back to the gym to look after Other Mother of Boys' youngest. Considering that she is regularly half an hour late (the record being nearly a full hour), I think I'm not doing too badly at only ten minutes, but I still get a look that could curdle milk. I've even got a parking ticket for this woman on account of her unfamiliarity with a watch. Grrr.

And unlike Other Mother of Boys, who is looking for ways to casually fill in the time till her husband comes home, I'm actually time-starved and chasing my tail. I would much rather not spend the best part of three hours in the gym every other day looking after her son when there is a perfectly good crèche on site. I'd have mine in there in a heartbeat. They do a much better job of entertaining him than I do. All this faffing about is seriously sapping the time I could be spending building the mumciergery (see, I still haven't had enough time to think of a name!). What company's CEO can afford to spend three hours chugging back lattes in the gym every day?

Feeling a bit narked by the lack of progress I get home from the gym and come over all proactive. First of all I need mums for this mumciergery so I call one up from the other side of the village. Hello Vera is a very sweet contact from my days doing good works for the local National Childbirth Trust branch. I was the newsletter editor, she the distributor and whenever we had a magazine meeting we'd spend 90% of the time bitching about how useless everyone was. It was good to vent.

She's a mumpreneur in her own right, as she sells alternative remedies – and Aloe Vera in particular, hence the name – mail order. She admits that it isn't making her a fortune but she enjoys doing it. However, she's pointed out in several emails before that she wouldn't be averse to earning a bit of extra cash here and there. She would make an excellent candidate.

Fortunately she's not up to much this afternoon so we agree to meet in the local supermarket café. For good measure she suggests bringing along JoJo Maman who is a stay at home mum also in the market for some extra cash. Happily both are enthusiastic about the idea and promise to spread the word as well as putting themselves forward as mums which, if you think of it, is brave on their part. After all, they've signed up to the service that has no name as I still can't ruddy well think of one.

Saturday 17 May 2008

The Husband takes Boy One to Legoland leaving me with the baby and some peace and quiet to get on with working. Of course the very first thing I do is stick on some useless telly, plant a baby on the breast and vegetate for the next four hours. Spurred into action by his call to say he is coming home, I buy more time by demanding pick 'n' mix (it cost a mint in more ways than one) and then dash about the house in a frenzy of activity, moving piles of clothes and scattering paper everywhere.

When he returns I adopt the expression of the world weary. 'God, I'm shattered, darling. I don't know where the time went. Between the baby and the website I've barely stopped so no supper ready and no tidying-up done. Wouldn't be a dear, would you, and bath the kids then pop out for a takeaway or something? I'm just so bushed.' Does this make me a bad person?

Tuesday 20 May 2008

The money situation is getting really precarious. Despite applying in March for a new mortgage and having the application accepted shortly afterwards (excepting the Husband's little blip which is still being trotted out as an argument winner whenever it looks like I won't get the upper hand any other way), there's still no sign of the money.

Admittedly there was a bit of a run on our new bank when they announced their rates because they were lower than the competition by a country mile. But so far every time I call up I'm assured that the funds will be in 'in just a matter of days, madam. In fact, I don't see why you shouldn't have them by the end of the week.' Many ends of the week later and we're no further forward.

It wouldn't be so bad if we were just plodding along with our old company and waiting to change over, but in their wisdom they've decided to give their customers a little push to get them to leave – by putting their rates up by three more percentage points. In real money that is more than four hundred quid a month to us. Or all of my maternity pay. Now, none is so willing to jump this particular ship as I, but it's not just a case of packing your bags and going. That would be too easy. This particular rat has been tethered to the sinking ship by its tail while the lifeboat sticks its metaphorical finger up to the wind and wonders if conditions might be a bit too blowy to go out on a rescue today.

It's frightening to see how quickly you can get into deep trouble if just one set of bills goes up and your main source of income goes down. In the last two months of this we have run the Husband's overdraft up to the max, as well as both of mine. Most of the credit cards are now at maximum and on one occasion I've had to use the one that isn't maxed to draw money from the cashpoint. And if there's a quicker way to bankruptcy than that then I don't know about it.

I've resorted to vacuuming down the back of the sofa and the car seats looking for parking meter money, and every handbag and back pocket has been searched in or cleared out in the hope that a stray tenner may lurk unseen. I may even have to get creative with the last-resort tins of kidney beans and pickled beetroot that lurk in the back of every larder. How will Boy Two take to pink milk, I wonder?

Roused from this bout of navel gazing by the theme to *Fifi and the Flowertots*, I realise that I've got about ten minutes to get Boy One to pre-school. Rushing outside jamming arms into coats and packed lunches onto seats I'm stopped in my tracks. I've got a flat tyre. No problem, I think to myself. I've changed a tyre before. Sticking on the radio to stop an outbreak of sobbing from Boy Two, I rifle in the back for the spare tyre. Located easily enough, but how the hell do you get it out? It's got some kind of weird nut on the top but nothing to unscrew it. I can find the jack, even the screw thingy for the wheel nuts, but have no idea about actually extracting it from its base.

Gawd bless neighbours. Jack of all trades has a quick butcher's and realises instantly that the tyre lowers to the ground from under the car (who the hell thought of that one?), while Jill of all trades looks after the baby, who by now is at the very limit of his tether. In five minutes the tyre is on and we are off. I'm still about twenty minutes late for pre-school, meaning Boy One has lost a valuable opportunity to show and tell his Spiderman web blaster, and I've missed Boy Two's slot in the gym crèche, which will still need to be paid for.

Tuesday 27 May 2008

Running late for everything yet again I go screaming out of the house to get Boy One to pre-school and Boy Two to the crèche. All strapped in, I turn the key in the ignition: 'Whurrrrr-unk. Whurrrr-unk'. Flat bloody battery. That's twice the stupid thing has needed fixing in one week. What the hell is going on with this sodding car? It's new(ish), it's not supposed to keep falling apart.

Luckily, this time I am prepared. I dash next door proffering jump leads that I keep about my person at all times. My previous car, a Friday Polo (i.e. built on a Friday with everyone in a rush to get to the pub, or still pissed from lunchtime, therefore held together with sticky-back plastic and string and guaranteed to break down every 700 miles) must have kept our local mechanic in holidays for years. It broke down within one week of our buying it (on our honeymoon in Italy – just to be awkward) and continued to do so on a regular basis for the rest of its life. In the end I sold it for scrap after I lost the war of occupation with the mold in the footwell and had to jump up and down on the bonnet just to unjam the engine.

With a brand new factory-fresh machine I thought I couldn't go wrong, not for a few years at least. How wrong I was. Fortunately though, the legacy of my crap car ownership was not lost, and I still carry around a spare set of jump leads for the inevitable. Unfortunately, I have a habit of parking nose to the wall and so when my neighbour comes to have a look, he shakes his head.

'Won't reach,' he says.

'Come again?'

'Won't reach. You've parked nose in and the lead won't reach my bonnet.'

Oh jeebus and hail Margaret, what now? Remembering that the Husband had recently re-joined the AA at great expense because he found he couldn't change gear in Tesco's car park (diagnosis – nothing wrong), I give them a call. After much confusion with them pulling up old accounts relating to the Polo and swearing blind that the membership is now lapsed, they eventually find the car's details. And they won't come out. Because I'm not more than 500 yards from my front door, I need Home Start to get going again. This will be another £80, thank you very much. I don't think I've got that much change down the back of the sofa. Kidney beans for supper again tonight, kids.

To top it all, when I go to pick up Boy One at 3 pm, I get told off by the nursery teacher for not kissing him goodbye this morning and also for not noticing that he was under the weather. Apparently he bawled after I left when normally he scoots through the door without so much as a backward glance. Repeat after me: 'Bad mother, Bad mother!'

Friday 30 May 2008

Our new mortgage is in and not a moment too soon! In fact it's actually a moment too late as we've just missed the cut-off for the direct debit for the old mortgage so are in the happy situation of paying not one exorbitant monthly payment but two. A quick call reassures us that we will be reimbursed the extra payment to the old company within the next week but I bet they won't add on the 7.5 per cent interest for the pleasure of borrowing our money.

Now that the cash-flow headache has been sorted out I set about paying off various heart-stoppingly high credit card bills. Although I am careful to arrange enough mortgage to cover them, it shows how much the intervening weeks since March have stung us as my extra pot of money simply doesn't go far enough.

Now we need only worry if next month the Husband will be made redundant anyway, making the issue of paying the new mortgage academic since we'll find ourselves out on the street. I'd better order some large baby furniture just in case. We might need the boxes to sleep in.

Chapter 5

Postnatal Cheques

Sunday 1 June 2008

I think I'm dying. I'm sure I had an out-of-body experience while trying to feed Boy Two at 4 am this morning. On reflection I think I might have got a *teensy* little bit drunk last night. The Husband found out through a friend of a colleague of a friend of a … oh, whatever. He found out through unofficial channels that his grant application has been approved, that he will therefore be gainfully employed for the next three years. We have postponed our trip to the poorhouse for a little while yet.

In the time-honoured tradition of parents of young children desperate to celebrate, we got them to bed as quickly as possible and then drank ourselves stupid. I vaguely recall trying to tango barefoot in the living room. Details are hazy. I can only assume that's where the carpet burns came from. It has been some time – breastfeeding, pregnancy and whatnot

– since I have consumed a large volume of alcohol in a short space of time. I suspect my tolerance has dipped a little.

There are many things you forget in the intervening period between giving birth to one child, then the other. How you always start the burping before realising too late that the muslin is on the other side of the room, for example. Another is that small children are no respecters of a hangover and will attempt to make your life as painful as possible. All hope of sitting quietly reading the large print in *The Sunday Times* and mainlining bacon sandwiches is dashed by a hyper three-year-old demanding to go to the Donkey Derby village fete now, now, now, NOW! The baby is also squalling but, as I had to suffer defrosting expressed milk at 4 am (in not subjecting the poor scrap to 40 per cent proof breast milk I am not a terrible mother, just 65 per cent dreadful, 35 per cent distracted), in daylight hours he has become his father's problem. One look at the Husband's bloodshot eyes and jaundiced complexion tells me he is not savouring this quality time with his second son and heir.

I had plans for the Donkey Derby. Being the good wife and mother, I volunteered to help on the pre-school's tombola stall. I also anticipated floating through the crowd proffering leaflets about the mumcierge service and chatting up frazzled-looking mothers.

Stinking of day-old wine and barely able to focus, I decide to give the tombola a miss. But I can't do my heavy promotions bit either. Forget that I look like Zelda from *Terrahawks*, squinting behind very, very dark glasses and hardly a glowing advert for my super-capable mums' service, there is still very little business to speak of. It doesn't even have a proper name yet. Mumciergery doesn't so much trip off the tongue as let the tongue trip over it, particularly in my state.

It doesn't help that I'm having some real difficulty in pinning down my Partner in Crime. Since our 'meeting' in the garden, when much wine was consumed and many plans were hatched, the business seems to have stalled somewhat. There was always a weekend away, a christening, a family visit that meant we couldn't get together. Phone calls tiptoed round the subject:

'How are the night wakings?'

'Terrible, yours?'

'About the same, five times a night for a nibble and a nap. Was furious with myself two nights ago – little bugger woke and fed and slept again in a matter of minutes flat but my mind started going with *business ideas* and I only dropped off just before the Husband's alarm went off.'

'We tried controlled crying but he isn't having any of it.'

'Want to meet to compare notes?'

'Mm, would love to but I'm away this week and then the next week I'm looking after the terrible twins for my sister. Just got so much on, it's a stress. Work wants to know about my plans for coming back too.'

'*Really?* And what have you told them?'

'Nothing yet. Trying to figure out my options. The

Family Friendly Businessman isn't feeling too confident about the economic situ-ation and I think I make him nervous every time I suggest not going back.'

'So what do you want to do about …'

'Agh, got to go. The baby's just figured out how to get up the spiral staircase but hasn't figured out how to get down again, beyond using gravity and an insane amount of luck. Call you when we get back, yes? Lossa love …' Click, brrrrr.

We've continued in this vein for several weeks now and I'm beginning to view the calendar with a certain amount of trepidation. OK, so I can relax a bit now that the Husband's back on the payroll but it still doesn't solve the whole 'Do I stay or do I go' issue with my own job. The Husband makes enough to cover the mortgage, his travel to work and the household bills. That still leaves food, my bills (about several of which he is blissfully unaware), the kids' bills. We're scraping it with my maternity pay but as the government so generously gives us twelve months off but only nine months' pay, all that ends in four months. After that, then what?

Thursday 5 June 2008

With the doula training finally taking place at the end of this month, I decide that a proactive course of action would be to get all the business aspects of the venture in place beforehand. That way, the moment I have my certificate in my clammy hands I'll be ready and primed to go straight out and find myself some fresh fetuses (with their mothers attached, naturally).

Boy Two's failure to nap in any significant fashion any more is hampering efforts to swell the family coffers. But perhaps trying to wean him while designing a website is an optimistic attempt to multitask. There is now a light dusting of Quinoa on my keyboard and he's trying to perform a tonsillectomy on himself with a Tommee Tippee heat-sensing spoon. Considering our family GP has just diagnosed him with actual tonsillitis this may be a great piece of forward-thinking on Boy Two's part. However, his exploratory jabbings are also making him scream at a nerve-jangling pitch so perhaps we'll leave the minor surgery until after he's prac-tised on *Operation!* a few more times.

I have another naming crisis, but this time about the doula website. Is setting myself up as *The* Reading doula a bit presumptuous seeing as I haven't even done the course yet and was barely present at my own two births, let alone anyone else's? In the end I decide on plain old Readingdoula.com, on the basis that the first thing you'll Google when looking for one is 'doula' and the place you live, i.e. 'Reading'. Some births can take as little as a couple of hours (my first included) so I don't feel that I'm excluding potential clients in Sunderland by pinning my colours so firmly to the Berkshire mast.

There are quite a few doula websites that call themselves 'beautiful birthing' and 'newlight'. For me, it's all a bit knit-your-own spaghetti so I've gone for dull but practical. I'm beginning to suspect that I'm a bit … robust for this doula thing. My philosophy has always been a little less 'Close your eyes and channel your inner goddess', and a little more 'Clench your teeth, give a good heave and let's see if we can't get this baby out before teatime.'

Friday 1 June 2008

Following the skiing fiasco, it's become clear that if you're going to work for yourself, you're never genuinely on holiday. I would take the radical step of turning off my mobile or leaving the laptop at home, if I weren't so terrified of the chaos that might greet me on my return.

So we set off today on a camping weekend for a friend's fortieth. Along with jerry cans, ice packs, mega packs of baby wipes and a wind-up radio, we bring the laptop, the mobile and two chargers. I have a piece due for the baby mag and there's a suspicion I may miss the deadline – again. I don't bring anything to do with the businesses that may actually feed the family in future, simply because I've procrastinated for so long that I don't see how another weekend can make much of a difference. The Partner in Crime is festering in Cornwall right now anyway.

I resolve to make the best use of the 'dead time' in the car by trying to call the child psychologist, who I need to interview, while we drive to the campsite. However the Husband has decided on a short cut through the suburbs to avoid the motorway. Passing several schools at chucking-out time, our progress slows to a crawl as we are mired in everyone else's school run. Boy Two is dismayed by our lack of progress and begins to howl and Boy One starts on the 'Are we there yet?'s. We are a mere five miles from our house, and around 130 miles from our destination. I suggest to my interviewee that we ought to reschedule for tomorrow and thank her for her forbearance. Slumping back in the seat I mutter to myself that this is going to be a very long weekend.

Sunday 8 June 2008

I need to pull some strings to get noticed, I think. In my ill-begotten youth working in PR we had a few celebrity clients, which meant I was able to flutter briefly like a moth around the brightly burning fame flame. I've propped up a very drunk BBC chat-show host while he drooled over a girl band, had my bum pinched by a US bad-boy rap star and driven around the Edinburgh Festival Fringe at 10 am with an aged comedian off the telly in the back of my father's equally aged Passat, complete with pint of beer in one hand and a spliff in the other. Him, not me, obviously. There are many, many things you can get away with in front of the Edinburgh rozzers at festival time but being stoned in charge of a celebrity is not one of them.

When I rejoined the real world I successfully jettisoned the boy-band members, but sustained exposure to the rarified atmosphere of 'meedja' London leaves you still a satellite round Planet Celeb. Every now and again I'm whisked on to a programme as a talking head and I bump into celebbier talking heads and engage in jovial small talk. Through the miracle of the interweb, one has even become something of a friend. Not an invite-to-your-wedding, drunk-dialling-at-1-am kind of friend, but friendly none the less. I'm not quite sure why she is a celebrity and she's not up there with Madonna or even Mariah Carey, but she lives in a posh bit of London and the chattering classes know her name so she officially qualifies as a 'Celeb Mum'.

She gets in touch to ask me to big up her latest book on Amazon so in return I tell her about the latest attempts to make my fortune. She kindly offers to bung in an endorsement should I need one to boost the businesses' profiles. As all her children are heading towards secondary school I can't really fathom how she will endorse my doula project – if she can, the gossip columns will have a field day. Mind you the mumcierge service will be quite up her street so a few kind words may go a long way.

Thursday 12 June 2008

One of the benefits of getting your kids into child modelling is that you can often end up with some fabulous portraits at no expense to yourself. However, as with everything in this great mumpreneurial empire I'm growing for myself, my bouncing babes have not so much as grimaced at a telephoto lens yet. With the grandparents lacking in pretty pictures of Boy Two to match the ones a local studio took of his big brother a year or so ago, I'm forced to take the baby off to the local snapper for a few shots.

It is one of these voucher deals where they give you a one-hour session and the first print for so little it may as well be free, on the understanding that you'll be so besotted with the pictures you'll feel compelled to spend a small fortune on several more shots. I have to take Other Mother of Boys with me to the viewing session because I know that, left to my own devices, I'll buy the lot and we'll have to live in a tent under the railway arches. Very practical is Other Mother of Boys, so much so that I have to rein her in at one point while she is enthusiastically binning every shot of my gorgeous boy. The sales chappie is shooting her evil glances by the end of the session as her barked dismissals draw him further and further away from this month's sales target.

Eventually we leave the studio satisfied a good deal has been done. Me, with several hundred pounds' worth of prints (totalling four separate pictures – I said it was expensive); the owner, with a palpable sense of relief that I've taken the commission annihilator off his premises. I make a mental note to push the child modelling idea forward a bit further. Boy One is growing up fast and it is Persil's turn to pay for the pix.

Tuesday 17 June 2008

I'm supposed to be a go-getting businesswoman. People listen to what I have to say on the radio. So how come I turn into a jabbering schoolgirl in front of my son's pre-school teacher? I come rushing in, all arms and legs flailing, show and tells forgotten, *verboten* peanut butter in the packed lunch, no hat or suncream. I couldn't organise my way out of a paper bag.

Wednesday 18 June 2008

Daytime television and a fridge full of white wine is the undoing of the mumpreneur. After getting Boy One off to school and, eventually, Boy Two off to sleep, I accidentally fall into a bottle of white wine. By 2 pm, and feeling ever so slightly merry, I actually begin to find the horseracing from Royal Ascot interesting. I have a vested interest in watching the fillies – and the horses – as the Husband has booked us the day out there on Saturday. His work has given him discounted tickets to the cheap seats and he is so excited about going to see some 'society'. I don't have the heart to tell him that it isn't called 'Chavscot' for nothing. I also decline to remind him that, writing for a marketing magazine, we're always being sent corporate tickets to go and watch so-and-so electronics company demonstrate why drinking fizz and watching gee-gees run around in circles is totally up with their brand values. A bit of arch-ligging would surely have edged us into the Royal Enclosure. If I don't go back to the day job I have to admit that's one of the things I'll miss. That and the Christmas hampers of 'the best our clients have to offer' from the ad agencies. One of them is great, as they look after Woolworths (a kilo of pick 'n' mix), Gordon's (a litre of gin), Baileys (another litre) and Audi (OK, a funny branded magnifier thingy rather than an actual car, but Boy One loved it in his Christmas stocking. No one said Santa wasn't cheap).

But this time round, cheap seats it is and so, under the influence of several of the nanny state's naughty, naughty winey units, I go upstairs rather unsteadily to try on some outfits. Halfway through my mini catwalk show I discover too late that the amount of energy required to get you into a dress is roughly half what it takes for you to get out of it again. Having wedged myself into a posh dress, the reality of having to walk drunkenly up the road in it to fetch Boy One from the childminder dawns on me when I realise I don't really have enough energy, coordination or sobriety to get out of it again.

In the end, I manage to return to jeans and a t-shirt after much huffing and puffing. Before Chavscot the seams of Posh Dress will, however, require some attention with a needle and thread.

Thursday 19 June 2008

With just under a week to go, I've been putting off phoning the people about my doula course. I haven't really contemplated what I am going to do with Boy Two for three days. Since our success on the bottle at six weeks, as I schussed down the mountain now and again, nipple confusion has reared its ugly head. I'm surprised that boys can even get confused about nipples. I've never met a boy who didn't know what to do with them. But it seems that too much switching about between teats and boobs gets them all aflutter when confronted with a fake boobie. So far, Boy Two seems content to chew madly on his teat but refuses point-blank to suck on it. Normally, I'd just give up on the bottle, jam him back on a bosom and try not to poison him with too much Chardonnay. But, the doula course is about 15 miles away and, elastic as my nips are, it's a bloody long way to stretch.

I call the founders of the course to explain my predicament and they're very understanding but are adamant that, on a course about babies, I simply can't bring one along. 'Too distracting,' they insist. I mull over the possibility of postponing until he's happy with a cup. However, looking at the list of dates the woman sends me I quickly realise that, as there is no reasonably close (and I count Manchester and Cardiff in that description) rescheduled event, then I wouldn't be able to start working as a doula until the middle of next year. This would put a rather large hole in my plans and a major dent in the family finances. I could potentially have handed Boy Two over to Other Mother of Boys for the three days but as she was recently told off by the desk harpie at our gym for allowing my son to scream his head off in the café for the best part of an hour, I think I should plump for something a bit more formal. I organise a horrendously complex childcare arrangement for the un-weaned one and agree to go it alone.

Friday 20 June 2008

I have been sent some pre-course 'homework' to complete before Wednesday. It doesn't ask any tricky questions such as 'How quickly does a unit of alcohol enter breast milk and then leave again?' (To which I'd dearly love to know the answer so I can time the next drinkie.) But it wants you to waffle on about what being a doula means to you.

One of the questions is: What is your motivation for becoming a doula?

I don't think 'Money' is quite the answer they're looking for.

Saturday 21 June 2008

Chavscot is absolutely the right word for it. It occurs to me that, since I'm spending a small fortune in diesel traipsing to and from BBC Radio Berkshire every week for them *gratis*, I surely should have wangled a better position at the races using my 'contacts'. They could have at least found me somewhere a good distance from all the pissed-up Antipodeans.

Also, I won't recommend bringing the children next time. Not the bosom-fixated one anyway. The drunken try-out dress is a great success except when it comes to attempting to feed Boy Two. It has to be unzipped from the back, then I have to take it off one shoulder and expose a boob, while trying to sit upright on a picnic blanket in what feels like downtown Sydney on a Friday night. I try to cover my modesty with a shawl but, naturally, the British weather has a say and the wind whips it away. On more than one occasion I am left sitting wearing a hat with feathers, elbow-length gloves and nothing else from the waist up. Oh, the glamour.

We will also not be making our fortune through betting. We put the minimum bet (I think the tote man is a little offended when the Husband proffers 50p each way – and tells him the minimum is £2.50) on two favourites, which come in last and second last. I thank my lucky stars I didn't choose hedge funds as my main career.

Sunday 22 June 2008

I see in one of today's newspaper supplements that one woman has chosen to 'cope' with the school summer holiday by drawing up an Excel spreadsheet showing the whole family's movements in colour-coded sections. It makes me reflect that I've truly become a grown-up when I begin to view the summer holiday as something to be coped with, rather than embraced in all its wine-and-sun-soaked glory. I pounce on this spreadsheet idea and plot our activity, day and night, from now until September.

The results of my labours cause deep internal conflict. On the one hand my heart sinks to discover that, in the multi-hued key relating to each event or commitment, there is no entry for 'sitting about doing nothing in the sun and splashing each other with the garden hose occasionally'. Our days have been planned in half-hour increments.

On the other hand there are pleasingly few blank spaces which signify that I have to think of something entertaining and cheap to keep the boys happy, while guiltily failing to build businesses, make money and bring home bacon.

Added to my beautiful spreadsheet (and I am making it some kind of challenge to have no blank spaces at all by the end of the evening, frantically booking playdates and crèche spaces at the gym) is an ever-growing list of things to do. Sometimes it's a 'micro' list. That doesn't mean it's small, just that it's a list of all the things I need to finish when I'm feeling the need to micromanage my life. It contains gems such as 'fill hole in corner of shower', 'hem dining-room curtain' and 'update diary contacts page'. On other occasions, when I'm feeling very 'big picture' about life, I create a 'macro' list. This includes: 'book loft conversion quote', 'explore PR opportunities re: gaining annual salary' and 'lose weight'.

The problem with all of the above is that creating these lists leaves me with an enormous sense of well-being and satisfaction in a job well done. The only drawback is that I haven't actually done any of these jobs, just written down that I *ought* to do them. I can also state with absolute certainty that I will get halfway through micro job number one before being distracted by something ten times more important – a *Simpsons* rerun, for example. Then the whole list will be forgotten until next time, when a new set of tasks will be created. If Paul McKenna wrote a book called *I Can Make You Stop Writing Lists And Just Bloody Get On With It*, I'd be first in line to buy it.

Monday 23 June 2008

This credit crunch is good for something. My eBay items are selling like hot cakes. Businesswise the only thing I've made money out of so far is being pregnant, as my maternity clothes fly off the shelves. The Husband is glad that the money *v* clothes equation seems to be working in his favour for once, but is becoming perturbed by the looks I keep giving his jeans. I think he knows that I'm making 'Buy it Now!' and postage calculations in my head as he walks past.

The Partner in Crime is off on holiday again soon, for two weeks, and I'm beginning to wonder if I'm ever going to get the mumcierge service off the ground. She's also having a meeting with her old employer tomorrow to see what they can offer her in terms of part-time working. It remains unsaid in our latest telephone chat, but I suspect that she will return to the office job after all, leaving me – where?

Postnatal Cheques

Tuesday 24 June 2008

Partner in Crime and I finally get around to having 'The Conversation'. It turns out that work does want her back and despite the horrendously unfavourable terms she is seriously contemplating their offer. After all these weeks of waiting for a decision one way or the other, I find myself counselling her on what to do.

'I think I'm just being wet,' she says.

'No you're not,' I try reassuring her. 'Well, OK you are, a bit. Your boy will love nursery and he won't miss you at all. That's supposed to be comforting, by the way.'

'I know, and it is.'

'Put it this way, could you hand him over to spend the afternoon going shopping and drinking cocktails?'

'Hell, yes!' She laughs.

'Well, it's nothing to do with abandoning him in a nursery, then. You just don't want to go back to work.'

She agrees that she's ambivalent at best about going back to the old routine, but acknowledges that she's been in this job pretty much since university. Giving up a good, stable job after umpteen years is hard to do, particularly when the evening news delights in telling you that your house is worth 10 per cent less this month than last. But, despite the lack of enthusiasm for her day job, I suspect that there isn't much of a draw in working for next to nothing on an untested mumciergery concept run from my dining-room table on a budget that would deem shoestrings a luxury. At the end of our conversation, (ex)Partner in Crime claims she's still very much interested in the whole mumciergery business, but as I hang up I resign myself to the fact that I'll be going it alone on this one.

Wednesday 25 June 2008

I'm still undecided about how to proceed with the mumciergery without the Partner in Crime. Can I go it alone? It is supposed to be built on networking and legwork around the local toddler groups and mums' clubs. I can spread the word in my own town but she lives in the neighbouring posh town where they've got money to burn and she knows just about *everyone*. Where am I going to get that kind of knowledge now?

But I can't afford to spend today scratching my head and moping about the house. Today I go on my doula course. I am but three short days of 'breathe and PUSH' away from a new career. Naturally, the course starts on the brightest and possibly only sunny day of summer. Why can't I be out in the garden with a Pimm's? Instead, I'm sitting in front of the TV in someone's darkened living room discussing the imminent disaster about to befall the perineum belonging to the howling naked woman on screen. It's enough to put you off your tuna mayo sandwich.

I'm one of five women taking this course, and by and large they're a nice bunch. There are two older ladies who seem a bit like a feminist Morecambe and Wise double act. They're both nurses on the edge of retirement and claim to have seen it all. The younger of the two, a New Zealander in her late fifties, is very prim and proper. In a pie-crust blouse and cardie worn just so, she's sporting coral lipstick, a dash of mascara and a sensible haircut to match sensible shoes. If I were to think of one word to describe her it would be … navy. The colour, not the armed force.

Her compadre, though older, is the racier of the two. A close-cropped shock of white hair tops a thin but jolly face tanned a lighter shade of handbag. It's a face that says: 'I spent my twenties slathered in olive oil and lightly toasted on the Riviera from May to September. I may look like a knock-off Vuitton but, bugger me, I've had fun!' On meeting her I decide almost instantly that, were I to have to go through childbirth again (oh dear God, please no, anything but that) she'd be my doula. She strikes me very much as a 'Come on, dear, my soaps are on in a minute. Do get on with it' kind of person. I like her.

Next to the Kiwi and the Bag Lady is Bambi. I call her that because her big wide eyes and perpetually startled expression can lead me to no other description. At 20 she's also markedly younger than anyone else in the room. But she says she's here to help single, teen mums who have been disowned by their families and dumped by their babyfathers. Her fees are being paid by a youth worker charity as her pay barely scrapes minimum wage. I realise that she is a one hundred per cent better person than I am, and out of guilt I resolve to read one more bedtime story to the boys when I get home.

On the end of the sofa is Clueless Mum. I find myself frequently fighting the urge to throttle her. She has three children under three, two of those twins, so she must be doing something right. It's just that based on today's evidence I can't for the life of me figure out how. Our trainer walks us through the most basic aspects of labour and childbirth and with one of her children under one year old this is something that, like me, she must have fairly recent experience of. Yet at every other line she scrunches up her brow and sticks her hand in the air: ''Scuse me, can you go over that bit again?' Never mind that it's written in 24 point on the handout in front of her, forget that roughly 300 days ago she was in the delivery suite herself, she acts as if she were being taught quantum physics in Sanskrit.

But it proves, if nothing else, that our trainer is eminently qualified to be a doula as she is clearly the most patient person on the planet. She answers Clueless's questions clearly and frequently, though towards the end of the day she does demonstrate that she, too, is human. I spy her deploying some deep breathing techniques after Clueless fails to grasp that a doula may have to get up in the middle of the night as it's the most common time for a woman to go into labour. If she's up, you're up. Clueless cannot seem to understand that a labouring woman might be a tad miffed if you refuse to come round before you've had your Frosties and a bit of breakfast telly.

Thursday 21 June 2001

The first day on the course went well, and I feel very well versed in the placenta argument – to yank or let drop. Possibly more information than I've ever required about this hitherto unremarkable element of childbirth, but I feel equipped nonetheless.

Boy Two doesn't appear to be scarred by his first separation experience. Though he steadfastly refuses to suck on a bottle, preferring instead to chew it into submission, he eats solids well and appears to love his childminder as much as his big brother does. Gratified that my childcare selection has been so successful I am somewhat grieved to find that I am, in fact, replaceable and am firmly on the path to obsolescence now that both progeny are happy with their surrogate mother.

My bosoms, on the other hand, are not so happy with this state of affairs. I refuse to submit to milking myself like a prize Guernsey (though I'm probably in the best company to do so – do you think I could get a discount for providing an impromptu breastfeeding masterclass on expressing?) during the course, but eight hours with no baby to feed left them hot, hard and heavy by yesterday evening. The Husband was officially scared by them, avoiding physical contact lest they 'go off' like a landmine. The baby viewed them with some trepidation. Since he'd last partaken they had almost doubled in size and every time he went for a snack he was shot in the eye with a jet of milk. I am quite sure that many less endowed women would kill for breasts like mine, however I'm slightly concerned that breasts like mine might simply kill. Well, they will if one more white-van man takes his eyes off the road to ogle.

Bursting bosoms aside, the course is leading me to question whether or not I'm cut out for this doula thing. It's not fannies close up and in the raw, lack of sleep during 50-hour labours or wailing women that are the problem. It seems that, because Mother Nature is surprisingly bad at timekeeping, the baby might arrive at any point two weeks before or after the estimated due date. And because labouring women aren't too appreciative of merry doulas (I don't think they mind jolly ones), you have to be sober when you turn up for work. Not unreasonable. Except that as you never know when the whole thing is going to kick off, you have to stay off the sauce for nearly four weeks just in case. Now, I've just spent nine months in the seventh circle of hell known as low-alcohol cider and Eisberg wine so I'm none too thrilled at the idea of climbing back on the wagon.

Friday 27 June 2008

Our last day of training and Clueless Mum persists in the delusion that a labouring mother-to-be will be quite happy to wait until at least dawn before letting her waters break, lest it disturb Clueless Mum's beauty sleep. The trainer also suggests we might like to offer a package called 'Early Bird' where you simply install yourself in the new family's home for the first 72 hours after they leave hospital, just to do whatever they might need. Clueless just can't fathom that, though they'd be paying her nearly £400 for her trouble, she wouldn't necessarily be given a cosy bed and told to snuggle down and have a nap. When she's then informed that the national association for doulas suggests you charge no more than £150 while you're training (the average rate being between £600 and £800 for a birth), she turns apoplectic.

It's to the trainer's credit that she tries to explain the term 'loss leader' to Clueless, who is getting squeakier with disbelief every minute. 'But what about my childcare, my petrol, my TIME?' She is then stunned into silence by an example the trainer gives of being on the phone for half an hour to a woman distressed that she was going to have a surgical rather than a natural birth. The woman wasn't her client, and it didn't look like she wasn't likely to be, but the trainer gave up 30 minutes of her time regardless. Clueless just can't understand that at some point you'll be giving of yourself 'off the clock'. And to think that she's signing up for one of the 'caring' professions. Let's just thank our lucky stars she didn't go the whole hog and aim for a career in midwifery: 'It's 2 am! What do you think you're doing letting your waters break? I don't care if the contractions are every minute – go back to bed and call me after *GMTV*.'

With the prospect of month after month spent in sobriety weighing heavily on my mind, I was relieved that the last part of the course began to focus on being a postnatal doula.

Apparently you can do the doula thing without ever getting on the business end of a uterus. Postnatal doulas burst into the new mother's life a few days after the birth with all the enthusiasm and skill of a modern day Mary Poppins. Their wish is your command but essentially it involves a bit of light cleaning, identifying one end of the baby from the other for Dad's benefit, pointing him in the direction of the cotton wool and boiled water and telling him to get on with it. Best of all, it's no more than three hours a day, every other day for six weeks. A defined period with a beginning, middle and an end and the opportunity for a guilt-free gin or two at the end of an evening. The pay is something like £15 an hour so if you had two or even three postnatal doulas going at once you could conceivably clock up over £2,000 gross in a month. That is working six hours a day for six days a week, but it would get me out of the house.

At the end of the three days we all leave in a flurry of hugs and promises to keep in touch, help each other out and so on. Clueless seems determined to remain my bestest friend while I vow to myself to stay out of her way as much as possible. I even manage to avoid walking back to our cars together in case I'm cornered into making promises I have no intention of keeping.

Which is why my heart sinks when I turn the corner to the car park to find her standing there shouting into her mobile with her car bonnet up.

'Thank God you're here. My battery's flat. I've got to get my son from his nanny. Can you give me a jump?'

I can't exactly say no as the jump leads from last month's fiasco are still lying on the passenger seat as plain as day. I'm reluctant not just because she has so comprehensively got on my nerves for the last few days, but because the very, very nice man warned so strongly against using your car to jump another. He was probably just trying to guarantee future custom for the AA, but apparently you can suffer an electric surge when trying to jump a car that will nuke your car as well as theirs. The last thing I fancy is being stuck in a car park with Clueless for the foreseeable as the AA once again ride to my rescue (and potentially present me with yet another bill for hundreds of pounds).

Figuring it will be faster to get it over and done with, instead of coming over like a complete cow by trying to explain why I won't be helping out on this particular occasion, I attach the leads and hope for the best. Deed done and profuse thanks offered, Clueless then insists I put my numbers directly into her mobile phone. Oh gawd.

Sunday 29 June 2008

I spend the weekend finessing the website and stalking pregnant women. I keep having to resist the urge to run up to the fullest fecund bellies and exclaim, wild-eyed, 'Why don't you have a doula? I could be yours... . I'd be really, really good, honest!' However, I have just enough self-awareness to realise that as a marketing technique this is somewhat flawed.

Instead, I think I'll stick to the website and maybe a leaflet or two. The trainer suggested two tactics on the money/marketing front when getting this doula thing up and running. One, it is best to spend the first two years in loss if at all possible. This doesn't mean that your business should be haemorrhaging money, just that the set-up costs and tax deductible expenses should be outstripping any profit at that point. That's because this country's stupid tax system will not only sting you for the tax you owe this year, but half as much again for the following year – before you've even earned it! It's not too bad once you've been going for a while as you're effectively only paying one year's worth of tax at a time (half of the previous year and half of the following, ergo one year's tax) but it's a bit of a slog when you first get going.

The second gem was that you should aim to spend *at least* 10 per cent of your revenue on marketing. To be honest, this wasn't a great surprise but, as usual, Clueless went purple at the thought of money lining anyone's pockets but hers. I'm beginning to suspect that the Husband is on Clueless's side when I announce that I've just spent £100 (= one training baby or nearly 7 hours of pointing at a newborn's bum and instructing new Dad: 'Wipe that bit') on web domains, illustrations and widgety things to make the website look good. I've even got a budget for some leaflets but I haven't decided what to put on those yet. 'But you haven't got any customers yet. How are you going to pay for them?' he splutters. As he is oblivious to my regular devotions to the great gods

Mastercard, Visa and Maestro, I gloss over this bit, muttering something about speculating and accumulating, and offer him a glass of wine. This usually works when I want to manoeuvre him off the topic of my spending.

Many hours of Sunday night are spent faffing about with PayPal buttons (will anyone want to pay for their baby with a credit card over the internet? Better include one just in case), broken links and *mots justes* that skilfully avoid having to say 'your torn front bottom'. Eventually, well past my bedtime – which, with Boy Two still waking four times a night ought to be no later than 9 pm – I have my online presence tweaked to my satisfaction. Readingdoula.com is live and I close my laptop with a sigh, listening out for the first of many telephone calls begging me to attend a birth. I realise moments later that of course it is nearing midnight on Sunday and no one will call tonight. All right-minded people are abed, even heavily pregnant women with raging heartburn, so I heave myself upstairs for an hour or so's snooze before Boy Two demands the first of several midnight feasts.

I am ready. Ladies, bring me your babies!

Chapter 6

Developmental Delay

Monday 30 June 2008

Because the last day of the course was all about setting up businesses, advertising, admin and whatnot, it's left me filled with vim and vigour, ready to get on with setting everything up properly. True enough, I was on the case with the website before I got there but the course has revealed so many other things I need to be getting on with. I hadn't considered that I need liability insurance. I'm going to have to tour toddler groups and network. This in itself throws up problems because Boy One goes to these groups with his childminder. If I turn up with Boy Two he's understandably going to be a bit put out that the baby gets to stay cosy and snug with Mummy and he is cast out, surplus to requirements. That's going to need careful management, I think.

There is also the question of advertising – when, where and how. I'm a big fan of the internet and no slouch when it comes to making my own little websites. So much so that I did at one point consider becoming a webmistress. But, there are fewer doulas than internet whizzes so I'm going where the competition isn't so tough.

Part of the fear about setting up in business for myself has always been the tax situation. I'm convinced that the tax office exists purely to take every last spare penny I have. And I'm none too convinced of the fairness of a policy that insists it will have all of this year's tax and half of next year's up front, if you please. PAYE was so much friendlier. It didn't feel like the tax man was stealing it off you when you never had it to begin with. Much trickier to have all those notes in your sticky little paws and then give some of it back. They're my preciousesssss …

Having one of my habitual moans round at Other Mother of Boys' house, I discover that as well as being a top engineer, she's also something of a financial whizz and has to do all manner of self-assessment because of her investments above and beyond her salary. Baffled by the complexity of managing PAYE and your own tax form I nevertheless refuse to be outdone and resolve to tackle the tax question head-on. It's something to do while I wait for the pregnant women to quite literally come rolling in.

Children finally abed, I get stuck in to both the sums and a bottle of wine because maths makes my head hurt and I need something to ease the pain. After struggling manfully through receipts and invoices, it all gets a bit much. Fuelled by Pinot Grigio (I may have accidentally fallen into a second bottle by this point) and frustrated by the house poltergeist which seems to have stolen several vital receipts from WH Smith, I have a bit of a tantrum.

Details are a little fuzzy, but suffice to say all the meticulously catalogued paperwork hits the deck and I stomp off to watch Jonathan Ross.

Tuesday 1 July 2008

I emerge from my pit furry of tongue and thick of head. Not for parents of young children the luxury of a hungover wallow *au lit*. The dining-room floor is wallpapered (floorpapered?) with bits of A4. On them is drawn a timeline of how last night's fight with self-assessment went from bad to worse, starting with neat workings (always show your workings, I was taught at school) and neater handwriting, then descending via scribblings-out into barely legible scrawl.

I was using one of those 'do your own tax for idiots' books that get you to fill in the blanks, hoping it would save me the expense of an accountant. When your outgoings exceed your incomings on a ratio of at least 3:1, I figure this is admirably prudent. In the Helpful Tips bit at the front of the book it suggests you begin filling in the whole thing in pencil first, so you can go over it and add in bits you've forgotten, then doing it in pen for the final draft.

I'm therefore somewhat startled to find that my drunken

shenanigans last night led me to scrawl 'THIS IS ALL BOLL-LOCKS' across May's petty-cash column in thick, black marker pen. Complete with extra 'L' – for emphasis, I guess. Mr Tax Man is going to love that. Does a duplicate tax book – replacement required on grounds of drunkenness and hormones – count as a valid business expense? Is having to do it twice, because you were too pissed to make any sense first time round, what they mean by double accounting?

Thursday 3 July 2008

I have the attention span of a gnat. I'm still really fired up about the whole doula thing but somehow can't bring myself to finish off all the little jobs that need doing. I have yet to sign up to the doula directory (which is rather stupid seeing as it's one of the main ways to get clients), pay my membership to the national association and fix all the broken links and repeated paragraphs on my website. It's the same with the bathroom that I decided to build while pregnant. I didn't mind knocking down stud walls with a dumbbell, and found the challenge of tiling quite absorbing. However the thought of siliconing round the base of the shower, or sanding the Polyfilla, bores me and now, nearly twelve months down the line, these little things remain unfinished. The single ungrouted tile glares at me every time I sit on the loo. It would only take five minutes.

So instead of finishing the job on the doula front, I skip over to the mumciergery idea, which hasn't progressed much further since the Partner in Crime bailed. I decide that it's high time it had a website, and to have a website it needs a name. I'm quite taken with mums4hire.com but trawling domain registration sites shows that that's taken. What about mum4me? Ditto.

Then, bingo! rentamummy.com is free. That'll be the name, then. Have URL, will travel. For just £30 I have a .com and a .co.uk (not planning on launching in the US, it's just that more people input .com as a default address than .co.uk and I don't want them going somewhere else, particularly if some kinky porn site gets wind of it …) and can get started on the site.

At my happiest fiddling around with typesettings and fonts, I don't notice the time pass until a casual glance at the computer clock while I'm sorting out the site's time format shows I have exactly 18 minutes before I'm due on air with Henry K. For what good reason I know not, they've started changing the day he has me on. Sometimes Friday, now sometimes Thursday. All I know is it gets my routine all out of whack and now I'm going to be late.

On a good day, the drive takes twelve minutes. Leaping into the car with what smells suspiciously like a baby in need of a change, I take off at speed, praying to the beneficent god of the traffic light. I'm held up halfway by a dithering granny in a Honda. I used to know the marketing director of Honda when I worked for the branding magazine. He was always trying to convince us that Hondas were vibrant, whizzy, speed machines, that they could be really sexy and cool and that they weren't just driven by retired schoolteachers from Slough. He was right, they're driven by retired dinner ladies from Reading too. I feel like screaming out of the window: 'Don't you know who I am? I need to be on air in five minutes!' I make it to my chair with a minute and a half to spare, with no idea what I'm going to say when they open the mic.

After the show, as I let my blood pressure slowly return to normal, I shoot the breeze with Producer Man. Turns out that he wants to go into business for himself too, though it's more of a sideline to his real job rather than a substitute. He's planning on setting up a comedy night in the local town. Before I know it I offer to help him promote it, and find myself with another website to build, because with two children, two businesses and the summer holiday imminent I just don't have enough to do, obviously.

Friday 4 July 2008

Striking while the iron is hot I force myself out and about. There are four toddler groups in the area and I grab Boy Two and head out on my mission to cover all of them by the end of next week. The first is one that I used to take Boy One along to so I know a few of the mums. However, embarrassingly, I don't really know any of their names and they all seem to know mine.

I start out gently with a mum who I often pass in the street. We start off with a bit of small talk, some showing off with the new baby, and then I dive in with the rentamummy spiel. She seems quite interested until her son takes a forward dive off the climbing frame and she heads off to apply kisses and cold compresses. I don't think it's a good moment to press the issue further.

Moving on to another mum I know from a while back, she too seems interested in the spiel and asks a few questions, although she seems more interested in earning money as a rentamummy than in using the service. I also notice that although this is very targeted marketing I'm getting on with here, it's taking me the best part of ten minutes with each mum as we interrupt our chats with 'Get off there!' and 'Don't headbutt that nice little boy, it's not playing fair.' If I choose this as my prime vehicle of communication, it's going to take me till Christmas to get round the village, let alone spread the word further afield. I'm going to have to get some business cards or something.

Sunday 1 July 2008

With the first child there is a certain understanding that your life has changed for ever and that it may be some time before you return to normal service. However with the second there seems to be a determination to have life carry on as usual. That can be the only explanation for thinking it would be a good idea to take two small, wriggly, impatient, messy boys to the inebriated sloanefest that is the Henley regatta.

We have spent many happy fuzzy afternoons slumming it in the cheap seats at the regatta, toting a bottle of Pimm's in one hand and a couple of litres of cheap lemonade in the other. We've squatted on the riverbank, barely registering Olympic medal-winners as they streak past, and giggled at drunken corporate flopsies as they fall off their heels and, on one occasion, straight into the drink. Why should this time be any different?

Because you have two small children, you fool! This time we are even luckier as the Husband has managed to swipe a Stewards' Enclosure pass from someone at work so we'll have access to loos and everything. I learned my lesson from Chavscot and though my dress is slightly less posh, it is still smart and crucially provides easy boob access for Boy Two without me having to get undressed in public (you're not allowed a skirt above the knee here; heaven knows what they'd make of me stripped to the waist on a picnic blanket).

However, in their wisdom the organisers of the enclosure have put the bar behind the grandstand so the view is of rather a lot of scaffolding instead of any boats. As Boy One grows more and more bored we try to move to the riverside but discover we are not allowed to take drinks with us to watch the races. Worst of all, using a spot of bribery in exchange for good behaviour, we faithfully promised Boy One an abundance of ice cream to encourage him to schlep the mile to the enclosure. Naturally, there is no ice cream within miles – cue industrial-strength tantrum. Rain is the final straw and we crawl off back home again. Fun is highly overrated.

Monday 7 July 2008

Pop out for a coffee at the local supermarket to stave off cabin fever and end up getting involved in an impromptu mothers' huddle in the café. The chair of the pre-school committee wants to arrange some kind of auction of promises to help fund-raise for the school, which needs a new building, grounds, supplies – the lot. Rather than demanding money with barely disguised menaces, she wants parents to offer needed services to each other. The idea is that the person receiving the service then donates what they would have paid for bookkeeping, babysitting or whatever, to the school fund instead.

I'm not entirely sure I've got that, but one thing is very clear to me: charity begins at home! I require a number of clients to pay into the mortgage/Pinot Grigio fund before I even consider giving it away for free. I think my bank manager might object too. I'm also slightly concerned that if the parents are all giving babysitting away for free (or a token donation to the school – I doubt it will be my going rate) then half of my potential customer base vanishes overnight. Sorry, but I am not staring at anyone's perineum and staying sober for a whole month just to buy 50 quid's-worth of sticklebrix and poster paints.

Tuesday 8 July 2008

And already Boy One is undermining my charity/home equation. To raise money for the pre-school, they arranged a sponsored bounce. Thinking he'd manage a max of one per second (and that's good going) I put down all the members of the family – without asking them, thinking I'd pay up on their behalf because, as usual, I'd left it all to the last minute and didn't want the wee man to have the embarrassment of being the only one with two sponsors.

The little bugger notches up 101 bounces, putting me at about £80 out of pocket. Lord, why has Thou cursed me with a healthy, active child?

Wednesday 9 July 2008

The first in a long month of Wednesdays. The Very Capable Childminder has thoughtlessly gone on holiday leaving me with both boys to deal with on my own for a whole two and a half days at a time. Normally, the relief with which I drop Boy One off at school on Wednesday is palpable. He goes to pre-school for two and a half days a week (it's all the Chancellor will cough up for) and then to the Very Capable Childminder for the other two and a half. Wednesdays are great because, though I drop him off, I don't have to go and get him again until 6 pm which gives me lots more time to go and get things done. Today, there is the flood of emotion again, only this time instead of relief it's fear.

Rather than just trying to muddle through, I decide that the only way to meet the challenge of actually looking after my own children is to tackle it head-on. I get Boy One home at lunchtime and launch straight into chocolate-Krispie making. I even let him stir, which I know will mean days if not weeks of early morning crunchy foot syndrome as the Rice Krispies cascade from the bowl to the floor and craftily avoid every attempt to get them with the Dyson.

But, as usual, perfect mother syndrome is short-lived and I plonk him on the sofa with the fruits of his labours and *The Lion King*. He's only seen it about 20 or 30 times so it's still fresh enough to keep him engrossed for – ooh – minutes, while I get on with some work on the rentamummy website.

I explore the murky world of search marketing, where you flag up a keyword and pay for how many times that keyword makes someone click through to your site. I think I've set the limit at a pound a day for a maximum of £30 a month but I'm sure I'll have a sleepless night when a bill for many, many noughts lands on the doorstep.

Concentration spans aren't helped by Boy Two, who isn't settling well at night. He finally goes down about 9 pm, only to wake again at midnight for his all-night, all-you-can-eat buffet. Meanwhile Boy One can take until about 8.30 pm to head off to sleepyville, which leaves me with about an hour to achieve all that I wanted to do in the day before I become incapacitated through tiredness. I do hope this isn't going to last much longer.

Friday 11 July 2008

Call our local Midwife Centre, which is where you go if you want to have a private pregnancy rather than an NHS one. To be fair, with the benefit of hindsight, I can't see how they will differ greatly. In 99 per cent of cases the babies get in there the same way, grow at about the same size, come out at roughly the same time and by one of only two possible exit doors, causing roughly the same amount of wanton destruction. However, must put cynical mother back in her cage and adopt smile of beatific, whale birthing mum as this may be where an inexhaustible seam of exhausted pregnant women lies, ripe for the plucking.

Boss midwife suggests I drop some leaflets round and she'll leave them out for the mums-to-be. I was kind of hoping that she'd jump at the prospect of creating a joint midwife/doula birth package for thousands of pounds that the centre would expend all its energies marketing and I would simply waltz up the road and do a back rub or two. But no, leaflets.

I hang up the phone feeling slightly deflated but nonetheless believe I have achieved something today. We are pushing forward with the business plan! Such as it is. However, it doesn't take long to dawn on me that I haven't actually given her the leaflets. That there are, in fact, no leaflets to hand out. And leaflets cost money. So, having crossed 'call midwife centre' off my list, I add 'get in touch with leaflet guy' to the bottom.

In a flash of inspiration I email Bag Lady from the doula course. While Clueless got on my nerves in spectacular fashion, I really liked Bag Lady. She had quite a wicked sense of humour and you could tell that she was probably the first girl at boarding school to sneak the form mistresses' sherry back to the dorm. Actually, I've got no idea if she was at boarding school but she definitely seems the type – jolly hockey sticks and all that.

But, disappointingly, she replies that she really has no interest in starting her doula career right now. She says that she went to the course to support her friend and mainly out of curiosity. Must be pretty wealthy if she can afford to spend £400 on 'curiosity'. She assures me that as soon as she thinks she might be ready to start, she'll be in touch. But that's not a lot of use to me right now.

Sunday 13 July 2008

The Husband has removed the children from the building with promises of being gone for at least three hours. I settle onto the bed and crack open the laptop ready to go hell for leather, knock the niggles on the head, get things finally up and running, and stride forth into Monday morning with great enthusiasm and yet another list.

- Call local National Childbirth Trust branch about doulas

- Spam every mother in my inbox about being one of my rent a mummies
- Spam them again to see if they need a rent a mummy
- Finish the doula website
- Finish the rentamummy website
- Finish the comedy website
- Update the personal website
- Draw up leaflet images
- Get business cards

I sit back and review my list with satisfaction. Yep, that's an effective day right there. Leaflet images, I think, will be my first task. A niggling voice in my head suggests that finishing at least one of either the doula or the rentamummy websites would mean I'd have something to promote, but I quell it. Making leaflets is so much fun and I get to mess about with computer software. It'll only take me about half an hour, then I can do one of the websites.

I've barely got Photoshop open before the Husband comes home, kids in tow, and I realise I've wasted the whole three hours on list-making, again.

Tuesday 15 July 2008

I booked a personal trainer session for today but wake up feeling all not bothered. However there is a very valuable crèche place booked for Boy Two, and seeing as they charge you whether you're there or not I decide to drag my backside down there and use the chance to work completely uninterrupted. I have my laptop with me and everything!

But their supposed Wi-Fi runs on donkeys and pigeons as far as I can tell, so I can't get my computer to connect to it, and their own computers can't cope with my interwebulator design program – which isn't exactly hardcore, but never mind. After shaking off the personal trainer, who is very puzzled to see me looking a lot better than I sounded on the phone (I cancelled with the full too-sick-for-school croaky voice), I get down to more Photoshopping, which I find truly satisfying but in the great scheme of things does not advance the Great Parenting Empire very far at all. A chance meeting as I leave the gym puts a very different complexion on things.

Bumping into the Glamazon and her family in the street, we start with the usual banter – off to the shops, aren't children funny, isn't it crap weather, sort of thing. Then out of the blue she asks how the doula course went.

'Do you have any clients yet?' she asks

'No, but it's early days. I haven't even got my certificate.'

'Would you recommend doing it?'

'As courses go it was interesting and I do think if I get my act together I could make money from it,' I reply.

'I'm thinking about becoming one too, you see – not that I want to step on your patch, but it sounds like a good gig.'

So, from being low on competition, it seems like there will shortly be another doula just down the road from me.

I briefly wonder if this is a bad thing, but just as quickly I realise that there could be a real advantage. Perhaps we could go into partnership (oh Partner in Crime, how quickly you are replaced!).

'Why don't you come round for a glass of wine and we can chat? I can show you all the things I did. Maybe there's something in it,' I suggest.

Glamazon agrees and we part company, untangling children from under our legs as they've been amusing themselves by using us as a portable climbing frame while we chatted.

Wednesday 16 July 2008

Despite finally finding a name for rentamummy and the interesting development regarding the Glamazon, the whole process of earning money seems to be excruciatingly slow. It's been weeks since I did any writing to speak of (which means it must have been a wise move to find something other than freelancing because it looks like the credit crunch is hitting commissioning editors as well as me) and I'm ever mindful that the maternity pay comes to an end in little over two months. Whoever I talk to about the idea of being a doula or of offering a babysitting service seems to think it's a great idea but the former is contingent on a willing and wealthy pregnant lady, while the latter – though oft talked about – is still very new so it's a bit optimistic to be thinking about paying customers just yet. Not that this is making the Husband happy, particularly when I return home once more laden with bags and with no obvious source of revenue to pay for what's in them. (The columnist India Knight says she got herself into terrible trouble financially a few years back because she would just wield a credit card and use it as if it were free money. But it is, isn't it?)

I don't suppose it's cheating too much to sign up at a couple of doula agencies in the interim, just while I get everything off the ground. I'm not stopping being a mumpreneur, just using the agency as a vehicle to get myself out there a bit. I do a bit of googling and find some local contacts so I fire off an email or three just to test the water. After ten minutes wearing my business hat, I have to take it off again and put the domestic goddess one back on as there is much baking to do, as ordered by Boy One's pre-school. Scared that they may have some clout with the next door primary that is notoriously difficult to get into and therefore catnip to every mum in a three mile radius, I strap on the pinny and get to work. I'm baking for sports day. Cook for victory! Ahem…

I meticulously calculate all my fairy cakes and bix to match the number of kiddies taking part, thinking that my good works will sustain the little Olympic hopefuls as they charge up and down the playground. When I get there with the booty, I am horrified to find that they are using the fruits of my labour as a financial enterprise! They don't want the kids to eat them, they want them to buy them. Admittedly it is all part of their maniacal fund-raising drive, but to add insult to injury I haven't brought any money with me so all Boy One can do is watch as everyone falls on the goodies, proffering their 20p pieces, while he stands by, sweaty and peckish. After throwing Boy Two at the Glamazon – 'Are you staying for bix?' 'Only if I have to.' 'Here, have the pukey boy, then ....back in a mo!' – I dash back to the car and scrabble beneath the seats, pushing aside sucked ginger nuts and dubious-looking clumps of mud to hunt for enough pennies to make a cup of squash and a fairy cake.

I am also narked that I went for quantity and everyone else, having a far better understanding of this pre-school parenting lark, has gone for quality and there are star-shaped bix with stix, fairy cakes of gargantuan proportions compared to mine, with jelly tots squished on the top, and dozens of saucer-sized chocolate cookies. I spent ages drizzling melted plain chocolate on top of my bite-sized chocolate biscuits and in comparison I have to admit that they look like small cat turds. It's unsurprising that they are somewhat overlooked.

Thursday 17 July 2008

I'm furiously cleaning the house because a) Producer Man and his wife are coming to do websites tomorrow and the house is barely fit for humans, b) Mother from Work, who sat opposite me in the office and had a scary propensity for getting pregnant at the same time as I did, is coming to view the bucolic country idyll I've been going on about. Right now it's a little more idle, a little less idyll. But finally, c) the Outlaws are coming on Saturday. I don't think my mother-in-law, a woman who bleaches the worktops every time she leaves the house, is going to appreciate that our bog is brown.

So this is the problem with working for yourself from home. Sure, the hours can be quite flexible and tea is on tap with no office politics over who made it last. It was you. Deal with it, and get the kettle on. But on the other hand matinees of *Diagnosis Murder* exert a strong pull, as does the odd cheeky mid-afternoon glass of wine. However the pressure of trying to fit deadlines and house cleaning into the rare moments when peace has broken out between the children makes this the only workplace where your tea break is taken up by spending 20 minutes with your head down the loo, descaling it. Between crusty bogs, website updates and leaflet quotes, it's taken me two hours to get one measly cup of tea. Bah.

And, in the end, it isn't really worth it. Producer Man calls to cancel our web meeting as it seems few people have comedy on their minds at this time of year. Well, in our area at least. I could have told him that the Edinburgh Fringe exerts a bit of a pull on comedy lovers and most are probably saving their beer tokens to see something there. I should know, I used to be a PR for acts up there. Not terrifically high profile ones, mind, but they did have their brush with fame. I tried to promote a funny show about Mexico by – and I always had to describe him this way – 'you know, that bloke off the telly who used to do the piano on that show on

Channel Four, well him'. In retrospect, that may have turned off more people than it turned on.

The show was good but it was at an odd time of day. We did manage to get a good marketing whizz, though. I persuaded tequila makers Jose Cuervo to 'lend' us a crate of their best tequila to be handed out to the audience. I've been paid in worse than tequila, although right now I'd quite like to be paid in anything!

Saturday 19 July 2008

The Outlaws have come to give The Husband and I some time off from the kids as well as giving me a chance to really focus on the websites and leaflets. Having Nain and Taid is always a joy, particularly seeing as the only parents I have to speak of are the Stepmonster (my late mother's ex-husband) and my very aged Grandmother. The former has always been childless other than acquiring me at eight years old. The latter was great with kids in her heyday but registered blind and unsteady on her feet at 96. She isn't in the 'ideal childminder' camp.

So having young, vital, enthusiastic Outlaws who are naturals with small children is a complete boon. But, Nain is so immaculately clean and tidy that I always work myself into a froth trying to get the place in order for her. Therefore, the last few days where I could have been working have been spent snatching every last minute to descale the loo or polish the microwave. And they aren't even staying here.

Sunday 20 July 2008

For the first time since Boy Two was born six months ago we have a chance to offload both kids and go and have some quality time to ourselves. The Husband and I spent last night planning what to do with a whole day of freedom but by morning it looks a bit redundant. The problem with the Outlaws is that they are pathologically late for everything. This is usually because Nain feels compelled to bleach the kitchen floor and worktops every time she leaves the house but for heaven's sake! They're staying in a tent.

By the time they arrive we practically throw the kids at them and jump in the car. We head for the nearest café with leather sofas (which defies logic as we have a cappuccino maker and leather sofas at home) and settle down to read the Sunday papers uninterrupted. Bliss.

Next on the itinerary is a child free lunch and shopping trip but the lunch isn't the treat we'd hoped for. Instead of enjoying a good chat and a munch, we sit in relative silence. Have we turned into one of those couples who sit in restaurants with nothing to say to each other any more. We could both live to well over 80. Don't tell me this is what I have to look forward to for the next 50 years?

On the way back to the car after a yet more uncomfortable silence, the Husband eventually pipes up: 'You don't want me any more.'

Well, that's a bit of a clanger to drop into the quiet gap in the conversation. 'Of COURSE I do!' I reply, a little over enthusiastically.

The fact is that I really do still want him in the big picture type thing, but right now he may be right. All the bickering, the sleepless children, money worries from him and me is hardly the greatest lubricant for marital harmony. I don't think I can tell him that though. It would sow a seed of doubt in his mind about our marriage that I don't really feel but that, for him, would grow and grow until we probably wouldn't be able to get over it. Honesty is not always the best policy.

Tuesday 22 July 2008

With the Husband at work and the boys with Nain and Taid I should be able to get on with the never-ending list of jobs that need to be done. The truth is that I'm squandering my time somewhat. Their time-keeping issues are having an effect too. I'm a bit of a morning person – I have to be with both children seemingly half boy, half lark. This means I function best in the morning, whether its exercise, work, writing, driving – I have to get it all over and done with in the morning as I start to go downhill after lunch. But Nain and Taid rarely get to the house before 11 am and after much perusing of maps for the day and at least two cups of coffee, they're rarely out of the house before noon.

I sound dreadfully ungrateful and I know that I am but I can also see chances to get things done slipping away. If I were a grown-up I'd just suck it up, get on with things and to hell with the afternoon slump. But because I'm a 34-year-old teenager I slope off with a sulk and plonk myself in front of afternoon telly with the contents of Boy One's treatie basket.

Saturday 26 July 2008

The week of free childcare is over and, despite my moaning, I'm sad to see the Outlaws go. So, I haven't done nearly as many tasks as I said I was going to – the leaflets are prepared but the website still looks pretty ropey. But I've had some much needed time to myself. I'd forgotten what it was like to go somewhere, even as simple as the supermarket, and have both hands free. It will be nice to get the routine back in our lives again but, as the Outlaws make for their car I find myself gently enquiring about when we can see them again. Is next month too soon?

Sunday 27 July 2008

The Husband takes the kids out to the park. Since Boy Two has finally got the hang of taking a bottle from Nain, I instruct them to be out all day. It's a scorching hot day and I optimistically get my bikini on but then plonk my bottom at the dining table and resolve to make no more lists (other than the ones I've got already), to do no more procrastinating. I'm going to meet each challenge head-on and get them out of the way.

Monday 21 July 2008

Yesterday was exhausting. I did as I said, and it's quite hard work getting down to it properly. Doing all the things you've been putting off, seeing each part through to the end even though you are bored senseless of it. I thought the day would never come but I'm even bored of Photoshop now. Lengthening my legs in last year's holiday snaps will have to wait.

It's done. Readingdoula.com and rentamummy.com are both live. Their pay buttons work and the download files download. I send emails to everyone I know who fits the rentamummy bill. I send pestering letters to local health visitors, annoy at least two women from the local National Childbirth Trust and I spend £200 on pretty blue leaflets to scatter like confetti across the GP surgeries of this fine Royal County. In two days, a juicy £500 maternity payment will scythe into my bank account making me temporarily solvent, but it will be the last but one payment that I shall ever receive from my day job. Then there will be a four-month wasteland with nothing but tax credits and child benefit to keep the wolf from the door. If my little, fledgling concerns don't fly soon, will the penniless reality weaken my resolve and send me back to work, cap in hand?

My motivation isn't helped by the fact that it is a swelteringly hot day and Other Mother of Boys has left two messages on the answer phone asking if I would like to join her for afternoon wine. Of course I would but I must keep going. For a change both children are passed out asleep in the living room so I have two hours to myself. Even though I don't have them yet, I send an email to the NCT's advertising co-ordinator about including leaflets in the shopping bags of the next Nearly New Sale. It's a massive draw for pregnant ladies and new parents from the surrounding area, and there's nothing like targeting people when they're in the mood for spending money. Like fish in a barrel.

Tuesday 29 July 2008

Over a cup of tea and the usual soundtrack of both our elder sons murdering each other, Other Mother of Boys suggests that a friend of hers might be interested in helping out with the mumcierge thing. This friend keeps talking about getting together a running-away fund. Her husband is something in the city and yet in their house his office is two breeze blocks and a plank of wood. To the outside world they appear amazingly wealthy but it seems that they have spent every last penny on outward appearances. She's a former model and air hostess and OMOB suggests that she could help on the party organising thing. She could bring in the contingent who have more money than sense (always a good thing). Mind you I'm not sure what a former glamour puss would feel about being reduced to babysitting and running kids' parties. It's one to think about.

Monday 4 August 2008

It's all too much hassle. I was trying to sign up with a local nanny and doula agency while I waited for my leaflets to do their magic. Do the odd job there (gaining some experience in the process), get the funds coming in and off we go. But the process for joining up is tortuous. Even though the agency owner seems so keen to have me on her books she's asking for so many references it's getting impossible to go through all the paperwork. I've photocopied my passport, driving licence, degree, household bills, CV, reference letters and it's still not enough. She wants something like four referees from four different jobs. Well, I'm sorry but I've been quite a good employee and found it quite hard to get fired with any regularity. It means that this side of the millennium I've only had one job, ergo one employer and one referee. At this rate she'll want proof of address from my primary-school teacher.

The current obsession with criminal record checks slightly concerns me too. After all, each one is only valid up to the day it's issued. You could have a criminal record check one day and then go on a mugging spree the next and to all intents and purposes you'd look whiter than white But, nervous parents seem to have latched on to it and any time you suggest that you're going to be working with children they ask for one. And I'll need to find another agency to get hold of one because you can only ask the coppers directly for a CRB check if you're going to process 100 such requests a year. Mad. I'll probably have to bite the bullet eventually and try to find a way to get hold of one, but if they're that important why does the police force make it so bloody difficult to get it done?

Wednesday 1 August 2008

Now, I'm the first to admit that although rentamummy is a good idea, it's not a unique one. There is an almost identical one based in west London. But they can't ply their trade here so I believe it's fair game.

However my printers have just made the almighty cock-up of sending the proofs of all my promotional material to the former treasurer of the local National Childbirth Trust. I am sure she is perfectly trustworthy but, basically, if she moves fast enough she now has all she needs to beat me at my own game and right on my doorstep.

I fire off an email to the owner of the printers, tearing him off a strip for being such an idiot. Then I phone Other Mother of Boys to point out just how big an idiot he has been. We conduct a fairly comprehensive character assassination for a bit then Boy Two has a floor–face interface and the subsequent yelling means I have to cut short the witches' cackle.

Tears dried, bosoms proffered, Boy Two calms down long enough for me to check my emails again, when I note another email from the printer. I click on what turns out to be the most contrite, sincere-sounding letter possible and start to feel rather bad. I reread my email to them and think that perhaps it came on a bit strong. That's the problem with emails. There are no grey areas, and however it sounds to you, it sounds completely different to someone else. My father and I exchanged a couple of emails like that last year and we haven't spoken since. But since his second grandson was born seven months ago he's enquired only once after his well-being, so this may be no great loss.

Friday 8 August 2008

The peace of a pleasant morning parked in front of daytime telly is shattered by the phone ringing. Could it be a client for rentamummy? Someone wanting a doula? Disappointingly, it's neither. It's Clueless Mum from the course in June. 'What the hell does she want?' I ask myself.

'I've got a client!' she crows, excitedly.

Groaning inwardly, I reply: 'Well done! How did you manage that?'

'One of my pregnancy massage clients. She's due next month.'

This is not fair. All through the course Clueless tried every which way to avoid putting any effort at all into the doula thing and now she's the first to snag herself a client. And it doesn't stop there.

'I'm really interested in starting up antenatal classes but I don't know where to start. Can I sit in on yours to find out?' She's obviously been on my website.

I should be flattered that she thinks I know what I'm doing, but I can't help feeling put out that I'm putting in all the effort and she's getting the reward.

'Of course you can,' I lie. I don't mention that the classes haven't had a sniff of interest so far. When she hangs up I turn off the TV and hit the computer again, determined to drum up some clients. Naturally, Boy Two chooses this moment to wake up from his nap so that idea is strangled at birth and I get on with playing 'Row, row the boat' and peekaboo instead.

Tuesday 12 August 2008

The printers' cock-up could have a bit of a silver lining after all, perhaps I shouldn't have been so quick to judge. Apparently my little proofs have been doing a circuit of their own. First of all they went to the former treasurer of the NCT who then passed them on to the current one. The first treasurer was actually an old friend with whom I'd fallen out of contact and when she gets in touch to tell me about the little journey my proofs are going on we get chatting. She's got two children now as well – one of each flavour and seems in fine fettle. A little more small talk and we sign off, just leaving it at that really. I think both of us realise that so much time has passed since we last spent much time together that it's a bit odd to try and pick up where we left off. I'm sure we'll bump into each other again in the future but there's no awkward making dates to meet that neither of us really wants to keep.

Then current treasurer gets in touch, admittedly a little confused at first. She knows the printer as they supply the newsletter for the NCT in this area, but cannot fathom why she's been sent these. After I explain she says that she did think it was a good idea and asks if I'd mind if she passed on the details to the newsletter editor as it would make a good feature for the new mums in the area. Perhaps I should encourage the printer to balls up more often – they seem to be more effective at doing the legwork for my business than I am.

An added bonus is that the box of the leaflets themselves actually makes it direct to my house this afternoon so there's no longer any excuse not to get out there and spread the word. The walking boots are primed and ready.

Friday 15 August 2008

Back at Radio Berkshire – I do wish they'd make up their minds about when they want me on, all this chopping and changing is making it hard to plan where to be from one week to the next. Crucial if rentamummy and Reading Doula are going to get off the ground. But I shouldn't look a gift horse in the mouth because I finally feel ready to get some promotion in for rentamummy and I need the promotional air time. I hand over a couple of leaflets to Producer Man and head into the studio for the paper review. We trot through the stories – why they won't let kiddies play in parks any more for fear of getting sued; isn't the American political system mental, but isn't it so much more entertaining than our own?

As usual we get carried away until, five minutes before the end, Henry remembers I need a bit of a puff. Having not really read the leaflet or indeed discussed the rentamummy concept he just plunges in where he left off with the doula info last time. He's convinced that I've set up a service to help postnatally depressed women. While I'm sure it could be of great use to them, that's not entirely what it's about. In fact, just describing it as a simple babysitting service would do just fine. I try to turn the discussion away from the depression aspect but it seems stuck there. It's unfortunate because it could actually be off-putting to the vast majority of potential customers. When they say 'there's no such thing as bad publicity', beware.

To make matters worse, when I get back to the car my phone begins to ring. Because I'm so busy trying to tie Boy Two into his seat with one hand and find my phone buried under all the crisp packets and squashed raisins with the other, it rings out. Missed call, no number left. Bugger it! It could have been a job!

Monday 18 August 2008

I took the doula course because when I looked online it seemed as though there were hardly any doulas in the area at all. Now that I've contacted what seems like hundreds of pregnancy masseuses, antenatal classes and maternity nurses, it seems as though everyone is a blimmin' doula!

I thought it would be a clever idea to try to link up with the local maternity services but instead I'm getting email after email back saying 'thanks, but no thanks'. Are there really going to be enough pregnant women to go around after all?

Chapter 7

Crawling

Wednesday 20 August 2008

I've pretty much exhausted all the places I can think of to promote rentamummy and the doula service. I've put posters in shop windows, handed out fliers to toddler groups, left leaflets in doctors' surgeries and set up website after website. I've emailed everyone I know and quite a few I don't and still zip. Nada, nuthin', not a bite, and I've been at this how long? It's been about six months since that first boozy afternoon with the Partner in Crime.

In that time I've gained qualifications, spent a good few hundred pounds, fought almost constantly with the Husband and Boy One. I've had several contretemps with Boy Two as well but he doesn't know that yet. He just thinks Mummy is pulling that funny face again. Is this really worth it?

Part of me (the bit left holding a shred of sanity and most of the credit card statements) thinks it would be a good idea to quit while I'm behind and prepare to go back to work. Pre-School Mum points out that most of us are in a pay *v* childcare deficit after producing the second ankle biter. She has worked out that, with two children three years apart you end up with one year where they both need to be in childcare. Then the older one starts school so you only need to pay for after school hours, making it only a little more expensive than when you only had one. But, I don't think she's figured in school holidays. I've been with my company so long I qualify for a goodly chunk of holiday – about six weeks or so – but that doesn't come close to covering the school holidays which total about 13. Even if the Husband and I never took a holiday together, we'd still be a week short.

Of course, she and I are talking money. I don't admit that the real reason I don't want to go back is that my job bores me to tears and – in small doses – I really do enjoy making papier mâché balloons and going to swimming lessons. I guess that the only option is to press on and hope for the best. We're still surviving on what is laughably called my maternity 'pay' and that doesn't stop for another six weeks so I can put off any major decisions until then.

After a quick half-hour of slobbing, mainlining ginger snaps and generally feeling sorry for myself I decide it's time for a bit more affirmative action. A quick scan of the local paper during my ginger binge reveals that the big agricultural show is on soon. We've gone before and it's a big family day out. A low energy lightbulb goes on over my head (slow to start, but quite bright once it gets going). Is there some way I could get rentamummy involved in the show? I've incorporated the doula service into the rentamummy website so I could kill two birds with one stone.

A quick pootle through the Big Show website reveals the organiser details so I put in a quick call. I wonder if there is a way to hand out fliers – maybe they'll charge me a tenner or something on top of the entry fee. Possibly they have 'goody bags' I could slot fliers into?

After much chatting during which we ascertain that I can't just hand out fliers (bad) but that the show secretary is much impressed with the rentamummy concept (good), we discover that I could of course take a stand (the table/tent/produce kind of stand, not point of principle one) at the show for only around one hundred of your best English pounds. Before I know it, I'm agreeing and we hang up, with rentamummy having just purchased 15 ft x 30 ft of soggy Oxfordshire field on a wet Saturday in September.

I started the day fretting that money for rentamummy was all flowing in the wrong direction (i.e. out) and that little return appears to be had so far. We end the day flinging yet more money at it, and this won't be the end. After all, you can have a stand but what do you put on it? Do I need to sell things, print things, give things away? Shall I just stand there and hand out pound coins?

Friday 22 August 2008

Once the shock has worn off of accidentally spending more

than a hundred quid on a stand at the local agricultural show with no real plan as to how best to use it, I get quite used to the idea of spending money to make money. This can be the only explanation for throwing yet more money at the project. With rentamummy/Readingdoula's joint turnover currently running somewhere around minus £600, I decide now would be a good time to invest in some advertising.

The local rag has a 'feature' entitled 'Bumps, Babies and Toddlers'. As all local weeklies tend to be, this one is fuelled by masses and masses of advertorial – a polite way of saying: 'Buy two ads and we'll put in some editorial that looks like journalism but is in fact just another, really wordy ad.' Preliminary enquiries reveal that they would like a hundred pounds or so for two teeny, tiny ads running in September and October that would entitle me to around 250 words of editorial puffery of my choosing. I'm getting quite used to throwing money at the business now so, on finding out that the paper is published just a day before the Big Show, I sign up.

Hanging up the telephone after my conversation with the advertising department I have the satisfying sensation of having done some 'work'. But herein lies the difference between those who work for others and those who work for themselves. Had I been taking the corporate shilling, ensconced in an office and waiting for the 5 pm bell to ring, what I had just achieved would indeed have been classed as work. I would have performed a task that, added to the tasks performed by functionaries in other departments, would combine ultimately to make the company money.

However, as a self-employed person, the task that I have just accomplished brings me no direct income today, this minute. In fact it has achieved quite the opposite and diluted still further my enterprise's paltry resources. I have done work, but it is currently unproductive work. It is still not paying-the-mortgage work. And for this reason it is worrying work.

I have a list (there it is again) of things to do that might conceivably come under the heading 'productive work' but for some reason I feel incapable of tackling it. By and large they are small tasks:

1. Go to local baby coffee morning to talk to mums-to-be
2. Fill in profile on doula association website
3. Go to Citizens' Advice Bureau to find out if there are grants, etc. to sustain family before profit is had
4. Fix broken links on website

But somehow these tasks, and many others like them, strike me as somewhat tedious, or they involve application, or they lack excitement. So instead of doing them I go off and do insane, exciting things such as signing up for the county's biggest agricultural show. I should know that I'm prone to flights of fancy. The Husband went on a business trip to Birmingham (the glamour) three days before I was due to go back to work after maternity leave with Boy One. The house was chaos, my work wardrobe in a crumpled heap and the paperwork out of control. With only three days of peace and quiet remaining before rejoining the rat race, I naturally spent them buying a whole new set of bedroom furniture, which needed me to build it from scratch, and repainting the whole room with a completely new colour scheme. Single-handed and with a one-year-old to look after. I couldn't find the time to put the washing away or empty the dishwasher. I could be a one-woman *Changing Rooms*.

My struggle with the mundane is to be postponed, however, as we are due to leave for north Wales and a break with the Outlaws this evening. As soon as the Husband returns from work, we are to bundle the children into the car and set off on our journey of four, five or six hours depending on the state of Spaghetti Junction. I've been promised that the Outlaws will entertain the children this weekend, giving me time to focus on the business. For the next few hours all I can do is arrange packing and then sit trapped in a metal box with no Wi-Fi – no website updates and no emails to chase. For a little while at least, with the Husband arguing over the map and the kids complaining loudly in the back, I can relax.

Saturday 23 August 2008

If there was ever a place to set up a business it has to be north Wales. Nothing to do with the piles of natural resources, cheap real estate and even cheaper labour. No, it's the fact that it rains – constantly. No pesky sunshine to entice you up Snowdon, no gentle breeze compelling you to take a bracing walk down the beach at Harlech. Plenty of lashing rain and howling wind to keep you indoors and tap, tap, tapping away at the computer.

Except today, when six months of nothing dictate that I should be hard at it, the Gwynedd countryside throws a spanner in the works and produces the most glorious sunshine in months. Bugger.

Our pilgrimage to the Husband's home town of Caernarfon is a regular thing – even more so since the children came along, although since the Husband regresses to a 14-year-old the moment we cross the threshold I'm not sure who is here to be looked after, him or the grandchildren. These visits are filled with trips to Electric Mountain, the eco-theme park, one of the many medieval castles or the beach on a rare rain-free day. For the last four years I have somehow contrived to be either working or vastly pregnant and so most times Boy One, and more recently Boy Two as well, their dad and the Outlaws go off exploring together and leave me prostrate on the sofa equipped variously with a remote control or a laptop.

As we drove up the motorway last night I had visions of more of the same for this weekend. Perhaps it is the unexpectedness of sunshine in north Wales, or an extended sugar rush from a four-hour fruit pastille binge in the car on the way up, or a sense of gay abandon that says to me: 'Hey, you've waited six months to make any money, what difference will another day make?' Either way, the woman from rentamummy she say, *YES!* to going out with the family and to hell with website updates.

And so that is how I find myself sitting on a quaint steam train in Blaenau Ffestiniog station with a mint choc chip ice cream. In the pissing rain.

Sunday 24 August 2008

Once again it's a sunny day, but as evidenced by yesterday's meteorological treachery I decide to stick to the plan. The Outlaws are dispatched with orders to 'have fun' with the children while the Husband and I sit silently on separate sofas tapping away on laptops. Him, updating his presentation for an upcoming business trip to Norway. Me, removing glitches from the Readingdoula website – of which there turn out to be many. Could this be why we haven't had many interested parties? 'If she can't manage a comments form, what's she going to be like faced with a breech birth?'

Later that day …

We're going to the pub. The sun stubbornly refuses to stop shining and I am getting screen blindness. A tentative suggestion to the Husband that we get some fresh air turns into a mini-argument about why I am happy to go to the pub but not willing to take advantage of some childfree time to head upstairs for a bit of how's-your-father.

Miraculously, neither of us manages to escalate the discussion into a fully fledged row, as has been the pattern lately, and after a brief sulk the Husband agrees that a bit of fresh air, and fresh beer, will do us both some good. The stress of his contract renewal at the beginning of the year, followed by the growth in workload from rentamummy, not to mention the trials of a new(ish) baby (Nora Ephron once remarked that having a baby was like throwing a grenade into a marriage, so having two must be like a full-blown declaration of war), has meant that we hardly spend any time together at all. We automatically sit on separate sofas at home, refer to each other as 'Mummy' and 'Daddy' and bitch about each other's lack of domestic prowess.

Walking towards the harbour pub the tension between us is palpable. Without Boy One to shout at, or Boy Two to fuss over, we actually have to talk to each other. Having exhausted 'nice weather' and 'wonder what the kids are up to' we fall into silence until we reach the pub. Nothing special in itself, the bar is just a typical old man's pub smelling of stale bitter and cheesy biscuits. On a sunny day, however, it comes into its own. Outside is the harbour wall which looks west towards the Menai Strait and the Irish Sea beyond. Most customers choose to perch on the wall, pints balanced precariously between crossed legs, rather than sit in the gloom inside. It's been a favourite of ours since before we got married and we always used to try to visit it at least once at sunset each time we were up this way.

Today is just one such day that feels like a harbour pub day, and the moment we reach the bar the old magic seems to be working again. A bunch of cyclists sit at the table nearest to the door, bedecked in tight lurid Lycra. A collection of strangled genitalia is guaranteed to make us both chuckle and it is all we need to break the ice.

Straddling the wall in the warm afternoon sun, the Husband and I begin shooting the breeze like old times. A second pint is soon called for and it tastes even sweeter (or should that be 'more bitter', since that's what it is) knowing that we are basically playing hookie. Pleasantly warm from the sun and the beer we manage nevertheless to head back home rather than letting the afternoon descend into messy misbehaviour. It feels like some invisible barrier has been broken and instead of our marriage stretching ever onwards to breaking point, it has been tied back together again, just in the nick of time.

Monday 25 August 2008

Having come to the parental sanctuary to get a bit of work done, rather than repairing broken website links, we've been repairing our broken marriage. All hail Nain who, rising with them at their usual ungodly hour, has the children both downstairs and breakfasting in peace. Normally I'd protest that as sleep is such a rare commodity we should make the most of it. But, instead of rolling over and feigning unconsciousness, I decide to go with our new spirit of togetherness and, well, get it together.

In the back of my mind is the thought that this is a pretty rare event and the last opportunity was more than a month ago. Since Boy Two, the normal rhythm of life has yet to return, both practically and physically. This time we are pretty careful, all the more so because last time we weren't. As I'm still feeding Boy Two there are no physical clues as to when is safe and when isn't. It may be psychosomatic but I swear I've been feeling a bit queasy in the last couple of weeks.

I should be enjoying a post-coital doze but find myself running through some calculations. More than four weeks since our last intimate encounter and no sign of my period returning, but then Boy Two is a greedy guts for his milk so it's not surprising. I know some women use breastfeeding as a contraceptive, which is deeply suspect and usually ineffective. That said, you don't often fall pregnant if you're not really trying.

Being a bank holiday, nowhere but the supermarkets are open. Even though I found out about Boy One in the salubrious surroundings of our local shopping mall toilets, I don't fancy discovering an unplanned pregnancy in Tesco's facilities. Packing the car up, I make a mental note to buy a pregnancy test first thing tomorrow morning. Surveying the amount of junk we need just to transport two adults and two children for a three-night stay, the thought of adding a new baby to the mix makes me come over all queasy again.

Tuesday 21 August 2008

I couldn't stop thinking about the pregnancy test all the way home last night. It will almost certainly mean we'll have to move house. For a couple, the Victorian terraced house is quaint and charming. With one child it's bijou, with two boys visitors comment: 'Don't you make a clever use of space!' meaning 'Christ, I'm glad I don't live in a shoebox.' With three children it will be impossible.

And this is timed just perfectly to match the credit crunch: house prices are falling by around 10 per cent a month. Even if we do manage to sell our house, the most we can afford will be something made of balsa wood next door to your friendly neighbourhood crack house. Having helpfully declared self-employed status to the tax office, our attractiveness to credit-shy mortgage lenders will now be on a par with Robert Maxwell's.

With the Husband staying at home this morning before flying off on his business trip to Norway, I take advantage of a childfree visit to the shops, including the chemist. I imagine his send-off at the airport: 'Enjoy your trip, darling. Bring back some Viking horns, salt cod and some newborn Babygros – you're going to be a dad again.'

Rarely enjoying the chance to pee alone at home any more, I don't relish widdling on a stick with Boy One shouting: 'Why are you weeing on a pen?' Having avoided a pregnancy test in Bangor's Tesco Extra I now plump for

Waitrose's customer toilets. It's a more upscale brand at least. Returning home I hand the stick to the Husband, who till now has been in the dark about my reproductive dilemma.

The colour drains from his face as he realises what he's just been presented with, until he notices the magic words 'not pregnant' in the window (I'd gone for digital for maximum impact on the reveal, either way). A range of emotions speeds through his grey matter, generating half-formed sentences including: 'You thought you were …? When did you think …? What were we …? How would you …? But you're not so …?' His stream of consciousness finally ends with: 'Thank God for that!' He leaves for the airport with the light step of a man just reprieved from the gallows.

Wednesday 27 August 2008

Now released from the shadow of an unexpected and frankly, at this point, unwanted pregnancy, I feel free to get on with getting some money in. What would I have done if I had fallen pregnant? Probably gone back to work to benefit from the maternity pay at the very least. But I'm not up the duff so there is no reason to cling on to the employer safety blanket.

Getting involved in the Big Show has given me a bit of a shot in the arm. I was really beginning to wonder if I could be bothered with the whole self-employment thing. It just seemed like such hard work for so little return. I have to admit that having no customers has been quite demoralising although why I expected them to leap out at me from the shadows when I've done hardly any real marketing or promotion escapes me. Because I've been bouncing backwards and forwards between rentamummy and Readingdoula I've failed to focus on either really.

Now, with the Husband away I can really get down to it. You'd think that with one pair of hands down, life would be harder. I tend to think of it as one fewer child to wrangle.

Sitting at the computer once the kids are asleep, I decide that rentamummy has to be my main focus. It's going to be promoted at the Big Show and there will be an ad in the paper. Yes, the money is vanishingly small to start off with but it's an easier client base to build and expand than Readingdoula. That doesn't mean that I'll give up on the birth and babies bit, just that I'll have something else to do in the quiet periods.

After an hour diligently firing off emails to Partner in Crime, Other Mother of Boys, the Glamazon, Hello Vera and others, I was actually working my way through one of my lists. Stretching to ease the crick in my back, I glance upwards.

Our home 'office' is actually a desk parked under the slant of the stairs in the middle of our open-plan living/dining area. Sit too far to the right and you crack your head a good 'un when standing up. The Husband and I have developed an instinctive snake dance to get up off the chair without cracking our skulls open, though sometimes in the rush to prevent a crawling baby from gliding down the kitchen stairs head first we get up too quickly and receive an egg-sized bump for our trouble.

Looking at the underside of the stairs, I muse that the dark wood is casting a pall over a whole room that is otherwise a symphony in white and cream (and chocolate stains and jam). The exact same thing happened last time the Husband went away. It's like some unexplainable force overtakes me and I'm powerless to resist. Before I know it, I'm rooting around in the spider-infested garden shed (I must be under the influence of some higher power as I'm extremely phobic and won't normally poke my head in there even in daylight), looking for a relatively new tin of gloss and a brush.

Thursday 28 August 2008

Woke this morning with a furry head due to not going to bed until 3 am. My right arm is also stiff and sore and flecked with paint. I suspect there is a large dollop of gloss gluing most of my ponytail together.

Boy One trots down the stairs to ask: 'Mummy, why have we got new stairs?'

I'm tempted to reply, 'Because Mummy has a startlingly low boredom threshold and can procrastinate to Olympic standard.' Instead, I say: 'Because they look much nicer and it'll make Daddy happy. Now eat your Cheerios or we'll be late.'

My endeavours last night resulted in a newly painted staircase, one kitchen door and half a bedroom door. In order to finish the job I have three more doors to start from scratch and two more coats to put on the ones I have begun. I will have to work day and night to finish the whole lot before the Husband arrives back on Saturday morning.

Because Boy Two will let me paint in peace while he plays around my feet, but won't give me a moment on the phone or the computer, I decide that the best use of my time will be to paint during the day while Boy One is at the Very Capable Childminder, and then work when they are both in bed asleep. Saner people would suggest that the best use of my time would be to try to drum up business for rentamummy rather than embarking on a time-strapped renovation project.

However, the Partner in Crime and Other Mother of Boys both pitch up on the doorstep expecting tea, cake and eventually wine. In the end the whole day is shot through with neither painting nor preparations for the Big Show nor networking for rentamummy (other than with these two and they're already sold) getting done.

Shooing them out of the door at around 4 pm, I have barely an hour before I have to fetch Boy One and the whole house becomes a zoo for the rest of the evening. In a desperate bid to prove to myself that I did get some work done today, I return to my failsafe strategy of spending money.

This is why I am now the owner of 500 white latex balloons with rentamummy.com splashed across them in lilac print. I'm not sure what I'm going to do with them but they cost yet another hundred quid so it's going to be good, whatever it is.

Friday 29 August 2008

Another fuzzy morning after another late night sitting on the stairs painting fiddly bits. The Husband is also making the surprise tricky to achieve as he insists on phoning the children every night over the internet using our webcam. Intriguingly he can see us but we can't see him. It leads me to wonder exactly what kind of Norwegian floozy he has secreted in his hotel room.

But the webcam points right around our main living area, from which you can't help but see the stairs and the kitchen door – now both a blinding white instead of a dark matt brown. I tilt the webcam around during our evening chat and the Husband wonders why I can't just sit still. I claim it's because Boy Two is trying to eat the webcam cable, but doubt I am convincing.

Never mind the Norwegian floozy, the Husband is beginning to suspect I'm up to something with the electrician. This is a coincidence seeing as I decided last night that all the electrical switches could do with being nice shiny brass instead of dull white Bakelite, and he is booked to come round today at 3 pm.

But, in a way, the painting project has given me some crucial thinking time and while mindlessly painting banisters I have formulated some kind of a plan for the Big Show.

Unlike many mumpreneurs I don't actually make something that I can sell. Equally, I can't just offer to babysit kids at the show (though some show-goers would happily pay money to offload them for at least a couple of hours). I need to do something that is very 'rentamummy-ish', attractive enough for people to visit and yet has no product per se.

So I've decided that the stall should be a microcosm of everything that a mummy does. Not the mummy who drinks gin at three in the afternoon and tries to get off with the only male primary-school teacher. Rather, the artsy-craftsy mum always on hand with some squash and a wipe that we all envisage we will be during the antenatal classes, before turning into gin-drinking, teacher-seducing monsters in the end anyway.

I'll get some helium (Ding! Another £100, if you please!) so that the balloons float properly and attract kiddies to the stall (if all else fails I'll make an excellent childcatcher). I'll get some supplies for arts and crafts and set up our camping chairs and tables for somewhere to do it all. I'll lay out change mats and wipes for frazzled mums to have somewhere other than the toxic chemical toilet to change the babies, and maybe I'll find some other 'mumsy' things to put on it. Then I can hand out these leaflets that I've bought and have no real use for yet and I'll sit back and watch the clients roll in!

Later that day …

Disaster! The people supposedly printing my balloons have just emailed to say that they don't have any white balloons and would forest green do instead. When I call up to find out what other options they have available, it seems to be that or Tango orange. I've just spent £100 on a helium canister and now I have no balloons to fill with it. Typically, the lead time on printing balloons being a minimum of three weeks, I'm at a loss as to what I'm going to do next.

But I don't have time to think about that as the electrician wanders downstairs to inform me that half the brass switches I've bought (only £80 this time) don't fit the holes. He'll have to come back and knock bigger holes behind the wires, which will a) take all day, b) probably wreck the surrounding wall and require plaster repairs, and c) have to be postponed for several weeks.

I take my frustration out on the bathroom door, painting with extreme prejudice and mummifying an innocent spider in satin-effect brilliant white by accident.

Saturday 30 August 2008

The Husband returns today and I am, at last count, two and a half doors, 500 balloons, one locksmith and a car service down. I am, however, one staircase, two and a half doors, 20 litres of helium and 40 plaster of Paris snails up, so I feel we have made progress.

We need the locksmith because several weeks ago I turned my key in the back-door lock and it snapped off, leaving a bit stuck in and the door stuck open. I have just been leaving it like this as I feel any burglar brave enough to steal from a house at the bottom of a dead-end street with a cop shop at the top deserves everything he can carry. And it's less effort than trying to organise a clear-out for the car-boot sale.

We need the car service because the oil light keeps flashing at me in the most alarming way, the right front tyre makes a strange crunching noise every time you turn left and occasionally the engine light comes on. The manual suggests this last signal merits the instruction: 'Turn engine off immediately and proceed to nearest Fiat Dealership.' How it proposes you get there once you've turned the engine off I'm not sure

I'm no longer concerned that the painting project will be unfinished by the time the Husband gets home because he rumbled me last night via the webcam. Interestingly, he didn't notice the stark change in our house's woodwork from brown to white, but did notice a sheet of newspaper under the kitchen door, placed there to catch drips. That he notices this in a house that looks largely as though it has been burgled already is odd but the surprise is busted so I'm in no rush to finish. In fact he can roll his sleeves up and lend a hand now.

DIY pressure off for the time being, I park the children in front of Saturday morning cartoons (yes, even the seven-month-old. Bad Mother, Bad Mother, Bad Mother), and get down to some computer time. Bambi from the doula course has emailed to suggest that a charity which offers doulas for women in prison might be grateful for the services of trainees so I send in my pitch. Most of the women are based at Holloway but they also deal with refugees and prisoners' wives and girlfriends (can you have a prisoner's WAG?). I'm situated between several high-density immigrant populations and also not far from Reading Jail so there may be candidates in our area. We were warned at the course that we might have to give it away for free to get started so I'm not concerned that I wouldn't earn much from this but it helps to get going.

Despite my best intentions, the Husband returns at lunchtime to the usual scenes of domestic chaos. Boy Two is wearing a nappy and not much else, Boy One is dressed as Spiderman and appears to be wearing what's left of a ham sandwich. The house is a tip, with washing both clean and dirty merged in a pile on the stairs. I have managed to hide the worst excesses of last night's wine frenzy which followed the spider mummification incident but there are many, many plates piled in the sink.

The Husband surveys the carnage, then his gleaming white staircase and asks: 'Does the back door lock yet?' When I mumble that this might have been overlooked but didn't I do a good job catching all the drips from the stairs, he looks thoroughly unimpressed. All the reconciliation from our brief stay in Wales seems to evaporate in a second and hostilities are once more resumed. I wonder if it's possible to mummify a human in gloss paint.

Monday, September 2008

Still fuming about the back-door issue I throw myself at the balloon question instead. After much internet trawling and balancing the relative merits of 8p per balloon versus 10p per balloon but two-week lead time I eventually find a replacement supplier. A fair chunk more expensive than the last one, but I guess it's clear that you get what you pay for. In this case, white rentamummy balloons instead of you've been Tango'd orange ones.

The boys and I have been invited to the Partner in Crime's birthday party, or rather the party for her son, who has just turned one, bless him. While he uses Boy Two as a climbing frame I bore her to death with the latest trials and tribulations of rentamummy, and the look on her face suggests that she knows she is well out of it.

As her other friends trickle in to the party I leave what I consider to be a decent period of time before badgering them into either becoming rentamummies or using the service. The Partner in Crime looks on benevolently, allowing my brief sales pitch to intrude on her tea party, but her body language is saying: 'Do you think we could get back to talking about poo now?' So I try not to bore on too long.

Being at a baby's birthday party kind of diffuses your anger after a while so when I get back home I decide to bite the bullet and book a bloody locksmith. I have visions of writing out yet another £100-plus cheque but in the end am pleasantly surprised. He pops round, gets out a scary pointy thing, has a quick wiggle and out comes the key with no damage to the lock. After 30 of your best British pounds he is on his way again. Had I known it was that painless I might have got it done earlier and saved myself some marital discord. Then again, knowing how the Husband and I are at the moment, we'd only have found something else to fight about.

Uncommonly pleased that I have achieved something that the Husband genuinely wanted done I decide to call him and let him know that Fort Jones is once again secure. His only reply is along the lines of 'Whatever' and for some reason that tips me over the edge. I've been slogging my guts out for days, weeks and months just because he was selfish enough to go and cure cancer and be paid tuppence instead of being something big in the city and buying me Mother's Day presents. And all he can say is 'Whatever'!

Fuelled by a dudgeon so high it's in the stratosphere I sit in front of the computer and fire off an email. It meets several criteria. Pithy yet obscure subject line so it frightens him into reading it ('I'm not happy'). Not too long or he won't bother reading it. Enough detail to make the argument watertight. Then I sit back and wait for his reply to see what he says.

Nothing. He says nothing. He's so tuned to the normal wavelength when he comes home, despite my monosyllabic answers to every question, that I begin to think he didn't even get it. Breaking into his email (which isn't hard, I already have control of his online bank accounts), I look to see if it has been read, which indeed it has. Looking up from the computer I can tell he knows what I've just been doing.

'You all right?' he says, not sounding terribly interested in the answer.

'No, not really,' I reply.

There's a brief attempt at a conversation but it's nigh on impossible with Boys One and Two clamouring for attention. 'The' conversation is left hanging in the air, the elephant in the room. The rest of the evening is taken up by putting truculent children to bed and fielding phone calls. In the end I decide it's better just to slink off to bed to lick my wounds. As I lie there listening to him watch yet another bang 'em, crash 'em, shoot 'em up film I seriously contemplate emptying the joint account, grabbing the kids and disappearing to the nearest hotel. Laziness takes over, though, and I decide to tough it out. Things should be better in the morning.

Tuesday 2 September 2008

I've come to the conclusion that the Husband is like sandstone. Rough around the edges, full of holes but not that dense. It just takes a little time for things to trickle through.

He has gone to work by the time I get up so there is no chance to pick up where we left off last night. I get on with a fairly unremarkable day at home, entertaining the boys, praying for the school term to start and titivating websites and emails without really achieving much.

To my surprise the Husband comes home earlier than his usual 8 pm, which delights the boys and surprises me.

'You're not going to leave me, are you?' he says, with what I do believe are tears in his eyes.

'No! Why would I do that? I just need a bit of help and

for you to acknowledge that I'm not sitting here on my arse doing nothing but drinking wine and talking about poo. That I'm not wilfully avoiding getting locks changed or clothes washed, and that maybe I just have too bloody much on my plate. But, no,' I half lie, 'I'm not going to leave you.'

I think it just takes a while for things to sink in and that perhaps the Husband did get the message in my email. I reread it today and it is perhaps a little on the strong side. There's no doubt I was feeling fully narked at the time but I can see how worrying it might have sounded from the receiving end! With the kids in bed we still don't talk much but there is a definite rapprochement. The dishwasher is emptied unquestioningly, I'm thanked for rearranging the bills and we even end up having a clear-up together, leaving enough time for a film on the telly that – shock horror! – even sees us sitting on the same sofa to watch it.

Wednesday 3 September 2008

It's been an emotionally and physically draining couple of weeks and as far as I can see it's going to get more hectic. It's at times like these I long for the chance just to sit and mindlessly surf the net at my desk. But, instead, I take the chance while sitting at home minding my own business, to let my brain gently atrophy in front of *This Morning*. Then Very Capable Childminder calls. My first reaction is to leap for the car keys, certain that my presence is required at A&E.

'What's he done? Is it broken? How long will the stay in hospital be?'

I've always had something of a talent for melodrama.

Fortunately there is nothing wrong with Boy One, who is outside in VCC's garden hunting for worms.

'Can you take care of a ten-month-old baby between 9 am and 2 pm tomorrow?' she asks. 'I would do it but it pushes me over my numbers.'

My first instinct is to think that she needs me to step in again, as I did with Boy One's friend in April. I'd love to help but I am due at the radio station the following day for my regular stint.

'I'd have loved to help you out but I'm busy, sorry.'

'What about one of the other rentamummies? Do you have anyone free?'

For a minute I'm a bit poleaxed, then it dawns on me. I'VE GOT A CLIENT! RENTAMUMMY HAS CUSTOMERS! Daytime television has anaesthetised my brain and I'm having problems working my head round Very Capable Childminder's suggestion. After all, I've only spent the last six months trying to set this up.

'Uh, oh, yes, of course. I could get on the phone right now.'

I hang up and realise that I have no idea who this person is that wants their child looked after, where they live, whether or not they appreciate that there will be membership and booking fees involved. However, I do a quick scan of the

ladies who have tentatively signed up to be my rentamummies
and fire off an email.

> TO: Mummies
> FROM: rentamummy
> SUBJECT: 5 hrs THURS 4 SEPT 10-Month Baby
>
> Dear Mummies
>
> I have a potential client who requires a sitter for a 10-
> month-old baby tomorrow from 9 am to 2 pm in her own
> home. Location is Twyford area. Could you please indi-
> cate your availability before 1 pm today, if possible.
>
> More details to follow shortly.
>
> Best regards
>
> rentamummy

I hit send and hope that the email looks professional enough.
I really should have thought about the nuts and bolts of how
the day-to-day business was going to be run. I haven't set up
a spreadsheet of rentamummies, I haven't sent out all the
Terms & Conditions packs to all the interested women, nor
have I figured out what the format of the notifications like the
one I just sent should be.

I knew there was a reason that being self-employed scared the hell out of me. I'm a very dangerous combination of utterly ignorant and completely disorganised. Vowing to hammer out all the creases after I get this little surprise dealt with, I sit down and start to make … a list.

Later in the day there is still a deafening silence from my stable of mummies. (Is that the right collective noun? Perhaps it should be a coffee morning of mummies.) Determined not to let the first-ever rentamummy gig slip through our fingers, I put in a call to the Partner in Crime.

Amazingly, she is free and willing to help so I call Very Capable Childminder and try not to sound too overexcited. Our 10-month-old is based about five miles from Partner in Crime's house which, bearing in mind the cost of a litre of petrol, puts a dent in her takings from the job but, still, it's better than nothing.

This probably isn't sound business sense but I decide to waive the membership and booking fee, just this once, meaning I effectively earn nothing for the last two hours spent checking emails and biting my nails. In a way I feel a bit embarrassed about charging these fees but I have to keep telling myself that I'm not asking mates for money and that I'm in this business to put food on the table. The model has been proven to work in west London and most people out here in the boondocks are actually on similar wages with similar standards of living so it's not like they can't afford it.

Crawling

Thursday 4 September 2008

By all accounts the sitting job went well today. Partner in Crime really saved my arse this time. She would be a real bonus in the business but she's set on going back to work and I can't blame her. Apart from the tasty £40 she earned herself today, the actual business of rentamummy earned squat. And if she had been a partner in the business, she would have been entitled to exactly half of its earnings. She would therefore have earned squat.

I still haven't had anything back from the other mummies about the job I posted them and that isn't good news. I'm starting to notice a bit of a trend here. I sent out 'keep the date' notices about Boy One's birthday party at the end of last term, asking people to RSVP if they had an inkling whether they could come or not. The party is less than three weeks away and I haven't heard a peep. OK, I've had three replies but out of 30 invites that's a poor, 10 per cent response rate.

Now that the mummies are also failing to respond – even to the promise of free cash (for a little labour) – I begin to wonder. Is it me – or them? I'm too busy with packing for another flit up north to see the venerable grandmother to deal with it now, but I mentally add 'Tell mummies off' to my list of things to do.

To try and clear my head I decide a mammoth walk is in order. I've got a presentation to do to a group of new mums down at the local doctor's later this afternoon but otherwise the day is surprisingly empty. The weather's nice and I'm feeling uncharacteristically energetic. Time for some exercise.

Naturally, as is my wont, I don't go for any ordinary walk. An amble to the park for instance, or a gentle shuffle round the village, perhaps to the nearby vineyard. I don't do things by halves and when I go for a walk, I walk. It's like when I spring clean. I don't just dust, I paint. Instead of cleaning the shower, I re-tile it. I don't scarify the lawn to get rid of clumps of moss, I tear it up and lay a whole new turf.

So rather than a potter about with the buggy, out comes the baby backpack, the suncream, walking shoes and bottled water. Extra nappies and wipes are located and then we're tooled up and ready to go. Striding up the road, looking for a good rhythm I set out on what is roughly an 8-mile, two-hour yomp across fields, streams and beautifully manicured golf courses.

We start well. The rocking motion soon sends Boy Two off to sleep and I'm left alone with my thoughts and the sounds of the countryside (swearing teenagers at the local school, the scream of cars down the A4, belching tractors carrying fruit from the polytunnels that have encased half of the county like a clingfilm fat wrap – so peaceful!).

However, it's been a while since I've done this particular long distance walk and halfway through my hamstrings are starting to protest, as is Boy Two who has woken up. He is attempting to draw attention to his desire for some milk by grabbing at clumps of hair and yanking as hard as he can. The pollen from all the fields is also starting to make life interesting and I'm getting into a viscious itch/rub cycle with my eyes. This is not as much fun as I remember it used to be.

Forced to take a pitstop in a field beside some curious and uncharacteristically brave sheep, I feed Boy Two for about half an hour before reattaching all underwear, backpacks, waterbottles and what not and set off again. Swollen eyes are making the walk take longer than usual and, since it's been a while, I even manage to get lost briefly, adding another half an hour to the journey. Five hundred yards from the train station I realise that I'm going to have to run if I'm going to make the train back to the house in time for my talk to the postnatals.

With a lope that barely qualified as a run I made it into town alive but not in time for the train. I tear – slowly – round to Other Mother of Boys' house and thankfully she's in. Despite being short a car seat she agrees to run me home, though she doesn't look too keen that my sweaty bod and cowpat covered boots will be in close contact with the upholstery of her sweet-smelling mini.

No time to change, I give Boy Two a new nappy and dash off to the surgery to see the ladies and their babes. The health visitor introduces me by giving a brief explanation of what doulas do:

'A doula will come and be an oasis of calm at a time when chaos reigns. She's there to support you, help you, understand and care for you. Nothing is too much trouble and after she's been, you should feel happy and capable, secure in the knowledge that you have what it takes to be a wonderful mum for your newborn.'

And up I stand, sweating, stinking, swaying slightly from the massive blood sugar low brought on by too much exercise, too little food and two breastfeeding sessions. My eyes have mostly closed up from the assault of all that pollen and the subsequent rubbing so I give the impression that I've just emerged from a marathon crying fit. I'm sure I look positively bonkers.

'Hello. I'm here to help you...'

Monday 1 September 2008

Finally the first day of term arrives and I fall on the pre-school staff with pathetic gratitude. Most suffer from a back to school feeling on Sundays. All summer I've had the same feeling except it's been 'Please God, when is he going back to school?' as I try to find yet another improving activity for Boy One to stop him pestering me while I check my emails.

After dropping him off I dash back to the house with Boy Two, having just remembered that the deadline for the puff piece in the local rag is midday today and I haven't put a scratch on paper. I had intended on trotting something out while up at the venerable grandmother's but what with children and geriatrics requiring food on an almost hourly rotation, I didn't get a lot done.

Boy Two miraculously cooperates and falls into a deep

sleep, giving me an hour's much needed peace and quiet. A period of frenzied activity on the computer ensues but with the punching of the send button I find myself suddenly at a loss for something to do. The baby is still asleep, no more balloons need to be ordered, no ads placed, no emails to chase (not ones that need chasing immediately anyway). I have nothing to do. I could go outside to appreciate the garden that I painstakingly planted last summer and have since left to grow wild, lacking the time to do anything about the weeds or the wisteria. However, my head is so full I think the only constructive thing to do is nothing at all. I park my bum on the sofa and let the soft inanity of daytime television marinate my poor tenderised brain.

I'm jolted from my peaceful meditation by the words: 'And now for the latest in our search for the ultimate mumpreneur!' There is no escape.

Apparently, *This Morning* is running a competition to find the country's top mumpreneur. Mixing elements from *Dragon's Den* and *X Factor*, they hold auditions and allow each mum to pitch her idea with a view to going through to the final. As with all competitions like this, most of the ideas are a bit bonkers but there are some that have you slapping your thigh and thinking: 'Bugger, wish I'd thought of that!'

Part of me is gutted that I didn't see the application form in time. I'm sure rentamummy would have been a great candidate. But then what would I gain from it apart from nationwide publicity (not to be sniffed at, of course, but there's not a lot I can do for you if you live in Auchtermuchty)? It seems as though the panel they've assembled is looking to invest in the businesses, which is great if you've got production costs and business premises to maintain. But what about companies like mine, which only want to grow organically? Karmically I may be about to shoot myself in the foot, but I'm not sure I'd want to have lots of money thrown at rentamummy.

Problem number one is that you're showing your business idea to the nation before it's got off the ground. What's to stop someone nicking it?

Problem number two is that they don't always know a great idea when it's staring them in the face. There was a mum who became a millionaire by making little doohickeys that you stick in the holes of those nasty croc shoes. I'm sure *Dragon's Den* would have kicked that idea to the kerb, especially since every fashion editor quite rightly tries to predict the demise of the horrid, sweaty things every other season.

Problem number three is that when a lot of money is invested in a business you get a lot of pressure from the investor to do things their way, or make the business grow faster and faster. So many people go bust when they try to expand too quickly, or stray from their original purpose because someone else is now pulling all the strings. I don't think I want that for my baby.

Right now my credit cards frighten me, the mortgage frightens me, even the price of butter frightens me. I would be most happy for a tidy lump sum to magically fall in my lap. But, if you were to offer me £50,000 for a stake in renta-mummy, would I take it? I don't think so. Then again, Boy One does need new shoes …

Tuesday 9 September 2008

A trip to the gym with Other Mother of Boys is supposed to take my mind off the chaos swirling around in my head. I'm so distracted I forget to take any gym kit. Despite the fact that these days I basically live in leisure wear, I decide that I'm simply not equipped for a trot on the treadmill. Unwilling to waste a session's fee cancelling Boy Two's crèche place, I stick him in the playroom regardless and avail myself of the club's computer facilities instead.

In between panicking about replies for Boy One's birth-day party (eleven days to go and still only four RSVPs), having palpitations about the Big Show and chasing long-forgotten emails that should have been dealt with weeks ago, I come across a column in the *Daily Mail*. And then my blood pres-sure REALLY shoots up.

For a start, the author calls our breed 'mumtrepreneurs'. Hey, you're the *Daily Mail*! Why bother with the accepted term? Spellng it wrong will obviously mean that you thought of it first. Dur.

Her basic argument is that as a group, mumpreneurs (sorry, I'm really not going to go with the extra 'tre') are trying to have it all. Working from our expensively decorated chocolate-box cottages in the home counties, we are largely sustained by our banker husbands. They're not all bankers, dear, but if you're using rhyming slang then you're quite close.

So, we have idyllic homes whose mortgages bother us very little, not that our husbands would allow such a thing to trouble our pretty heads. I'd add to this that we're all wearing Laura Ashley dresses with pie-crust collars, but we'll go with the more modern Boden instead.

Now, naughty ladies that we are, we're not content with staying at home and bringing up immaculate children. No, we must have careers to feel fulfilled but that travelling to an office is just a little, well, beneath us. So we park our personal trainer-honed behinds at the enormous oak table in front of the Aga and start running up darling smock dresses and pin-tuck baby blankets, which we sell on to our landed gentry friends at suitably posh mark-ups.

But, mumpreneurs of Britain, you should be ashamed of yourselves! Don't you realise this satanic activity is depriving your little ones of precious moments being bounced on your knee? How do you expect them to excel at Kumon or piano if you can't be there to supervise, and insist on doing your silly little hobby instead?

Does it cross the columnist's mind that we may be scratching a living from the kitchen table simply because there is no other logistical way of doing it? As the Husband isn't something big in the city (which, judging by the way things are going, is not altogether a bad thing) and I don't have a tidy little trust fund tucked away, I may have to work while keeping my children with me. As it is, I can't afford to go to work but I can't afford not to. Kitchen table and renta-mummy it is, then, you daft old bat.

Wednesday 10 September 2008

Less than three days to go and I am now officially beyond stressed. I have acquired 'stress insomnia'. For many the inability to sleep when they get to bed is an inconvenience, but for the mothers of small children who routinely get them up in the middle of the night anyway, it is akin to torture.

On a really bad night, they can tag team: one wakes at midnight and by the time he is settled at 1 am, the other gets up. An hour later they are both sleeping soundly but because your brain is whirring with all the possibilities – in my case, will the gazebo go up straight? Will anyone come to the stand? What if the face painter is crap? – you are wide awake for the next hour and a half. And finally, as you slide gently into the Sandman's embrace, a small voice calls out: 'Mummeeeee, I need a weeeeeeeeeee!'

Bastards.

Thursday 11 September 2008

As the day of the Big Show approaches I realise that I should really go to the ground and familiarise myself with the place I'll call home this Saturday. Following Land Rovers, horse boxes, lorries and quad bikes into an area that is less paddock, more quagmire, I sink down in my seat below my steering wheel, all too aware that my Multipla, otherwise known in town as the Big Blue Bus, now looks like a pathetic little city car among all the countrified heavy plant tooling around the grounds.

I pray the vehicles in front don't stop because if they, and I, do there will be a mortifying amount of wheel spin before I slowly bury myself up to the armpits in one of Oxfordshire's finer fields. Then burly farmhands and stable lads will have to come and help the little woman in her towny car pathetically lacking in 4 x 4 or tractor tyres and they will chuckle behind their horny man-of-the-soil hands and shake their heads and suggest I go back to drinking Starbucks and shopping in Gap and leave the countryside to them what knows how to deal with it.

Coming muddily but safely to a stop I scrutinise the incomprehensible ground plan for the show and look for my pitch. I decide that I've found the right spot and get out for a recce. I'd been quite pleased on receiving my grid reference to discover that I was really near to all the family rides, food courts and mini farm. This meant a good steady flow of passing trade. However, on inspecting the area, I can't see where one might stick a 12 ft x 12 ft gazebo. There is a big space reserved for a climbing wall, an even bigger one for the octopus bouncy castle (I have no idea what logical thought process led someone to decide that an octopus was de rigueur for a castle: 'Turrets? Check. Moat? Check. Portcullis? Check. Eight-legged sea creature? Check), but no obvious spot for rentamummy.

Then I realise that I am, in fact, in totally the wrong place. Embarrassed, as our horny men-of-the-soil now probably think not only that I have a stupid car but am also completely lost and was shooting for Starbucks all along, I slink back into the car and gently ease onto some slightly more stable ground heading for the right part of the ground. I should have been up by the trade stands covering garden furniture, every permutation of welly you can think of and the sweetie van. Not quite as much passing trade as I'd previously thought but it isn't bad. Finding my pitch I mentally plot where to put everything. Some of my neighbours already have their tents up, but as I have only a flimsy telescopic gazebo I don't trust the late summer weather to leave it in peace overnight. If I were to pitch it here and now I would fully expect to see it floating gracefully down the nearby river tomorrow morning. In anticipation of an early and chaotic start to the weekend, I head home via the supermarket in search of a little something to fortify the Husband and me for the next 48 hours.

Fully aware that rentamummy isn't going to pull in the crowds on its own, I know I need an attraction of some sort to reel them in. Other Mother of Boys recommends her nursery nurse as a great face painter and so the deal is done. She can have the stand space for free to make as much money for herself as she wants doing her face painting at three quid a pop. In return, the children's parents will be pretty much held captive while I trot out my business spiel. Now I actually have something to sell on my stand other than my winning smile.

Friday 12 September 2008

I have … the call.

This woman has been going to our local Midwife Centre for reflexology and asked about doulas. The owner gave her my leaflet and said I was, quote, 'a lovely lass'. Though this makes me sound like a Dickensian milkmaid I'm still very grateful for the plug and make a mental note to send an email thanking her for the nudge in my direction.

So a pregnant lady calls me and suddenly I've come over all of a flutter. First thought: Way-hey, here we go. Second thought a nanosecond after the first: Oh crikey, I've got to go and watch some woman's baby being born. Third and many more subsequent thoughts: EEEEK!

It appears that she already had a doula but after the second meeting this woman scared the wits out of her. Pregnant Lady's birth is due to be highly medicalised because of the amount of medication she's been on during pregnancy, previous interventions and whatnot. Despite this the original doula was a bit too hemp-and-sandals and determined to steer her client towards the 'whale song on all fours at home wrapped in Alpaca birth shawl' end of the spectrum. That idea's been dropped like a hot potato, and the doula with it.

Crawling

I'm getting the probing questions and dealing quite well with them, I think, gently fudging the issue of how much – or in my case how little – experience I've got. I impress with knowledge of treatments for breech (i.e. upside down and therefore very ouchy to get out) babies, stun with tales of writing for parenting mags and appearances on t'radio and t'telly. However, the inevitable happens:

'How many newborns have you attended?'

'Mm, well, I think you could probably, well, it's around, um … two.'

'Oh that's good. Whose were they?'

'Er, mine.'

'Ah.'

I go on to point out that I was very definitely there during the birth of both my own two boys and I was practically there at my friend's, just missing out on the gooey bit. (This is not strictly true – I am amalgamating the experience of two friends. Partner in Crime kept me regularly updated by telephone about her labour experience while it was happening and Other Mother of Boys called to cancel a lunch date and then mentioned in passing that her Boy Two had been born about an hour before. I feel that these two telephone conversations count as 'being there while labour is in progress'.)

Pregnant Lady isn't overly impressed by my birth CV and suggests that, as she'll be needing all the bells and whistles for her impending birth, a panicking virgin doula isn't really what she has in mind. I agree, though inside I'm going 'Bugger,

bugger, bugger', and thinking of this month's credit card bill. She doesn't rule out using me altogether but does want me to know that she'll still be looking for a more experienced partner.

How to break the duck is always a tricky one. The Husband suggests I 'shadow' another doula, but that would basically be like preparing one whole month's work for free – including the sobriety (I'm still having a hard time coming to terms with the need for that, even when I'd be paid for it). I could fib, but it's a bit tricky when it comes to references and I'd also make a tit of myself if my first real experience ends with me flapping about like a headless chicken. I've tried the more disadvantaged end of the scale, getting in touch with the organisation Bambi recommended, the one that provides doulas for pregnant female prisoners, and even they don't want me. It's just a case of crossing my fingers and hoping.

Anyway, I don't have time to worry about ducks and doulas. It's the Big Show tomorrow. List-mania is out of control and I am now toting three pages of chores with colour coding and jobs timed in half-hour slots. I have plaster of Paris snails to make, balloons to inflate and the Husband to drive into the ground. The irony that the Partner in Crime and I had the idea for rentamummy because we could do with a cool head and a helping hand now and again has never been more apparent. There is a new definition of frazzled and I'm it.

Chapter 8

Standing Unaided

The alarm goes off at 6.30 am and this is wrong on so many levels. For a start it's Saturday. Saturday shouldn't even have a 6.30 am. Yes, Boy Two usually wakes now – sometimes even well before – but I usually just slide him over, jam in a boob and we both doze off back to sleep for an hour or so. Boy One has a bunny that tells him when to get up, which the Husband regularly winds forward to about 8.30 am. Boy One may be awake by 6 am but he knows not to bother Daddy until Bunny's woken up. At least, he knows the short shrift he'll get if he tries.

So, naturally, this is the first weekend when neither Boy One nor Boy Two has stirred before 6.30 am. Because of the show, the Husband and I have been rudely wrenched from our slumber at stupid 6.30 yet both sprogs continue to snore on regardless. Not fair.

Naturally, the challenge of presenting rentamummy at the biggest agricultural show in the county isn't enough for me, so I arranged for Boy One to start a term of swimming lessons this morning too. As we sit in the three-mile queue to get to the showground, time ticks by and it is getting perilously close to Boy One's allotted swimming hour. Barely after we arrive, the Husband will have to turn around and shoot off to the swimming pool. My plans to have a willing slave to inflate 500 rentamummy balloons are evaporating.

Following my recce two days ago, we drive confidently towards my pitch once we reach the field. Unfortunately there have been a few comings and goings since my little city car was last here and the ground is even less stable than before. The convoy in front stops and I too am forced to come to a halt. As we move off again I cringe to hear the telltale whine of a spinning back wheel. A marshal heads towards me, his face on the 'here we go again' setting. However, before he reaches me, the wheel catches and we set off, slipping and sliding to our destination.

In the end, we make it to the stand with about ten minutes to spare. The Husband throws everything out of the boot, slings the children back in the car and speeds – well, crawls, slides, then crawls some more – off to the pool.

I survey the pile of 'show junk' gradually sinking into the mud, think 'What the hell have I let myself in for?', muster some sterner stuff and get on with building the stand single-handed. Balloons will have to wait.

What was once a big green field with a few white marquees is a hive of activity. Our plot, which was naked as far as the eye can see, is now squeezed on both sides by exhibitors busy with tents and poles and trestle tables. The garden furniture people are still there and little seems to have changed. As I look to the other side of my pitch, however, my heart sinks. A huge camouflage tent complete with sludge-coloured netting butts right up against rentamummy's border. The squaddies have arrived. Not quite squaddies – sea cadets on a recruitment drive – but judging from the language coming from inside their tent there is little to tell between them. Not so many cans of lager, perhaps.

I spent last night trawling the internet for the official logo of UNICEF's 'Baby Friendly' Initiative. This all sounds terribly serious, but the logo is basically shorthand to say: 'You are welcome to breastfeed here.' There are usually lots of stork-fresh™ babies in tow at the show, including mine, and it's not that comfy trying to get a boob in while perching on one of the artfully arranged hay bales. It's also a little disconcerting if you're sitting next to the main ring and the man on the tannoy suddenly booms: 'LOOK AT THE UDDERS ON THAT!' In post-partum befuddlement it's a while before you realise he's talking about the prize-winning Guernsey on the other side of the fence.

I figure that a good way to entice parents into my stall is to give feeding mums somewhere comfortable and discreet to do it. So I hang up my Baby Friendly sign on the gazebo and unpack those high-backed camping armchairs along with a few blankets for subtle draping. Also for keeping warm in case the delightful late-summer weather (i.e. horizontal rain) continues. Standing back to appraise my handiwork it occurs to me that, try as I might to provide a welcoming environment to breastfeed in, most women will probably feel less than comfortable at exposing their breasts when cheek-by-jowl with a bunch of squaddies.

With all the basics of my stall now up, I begin to wrestle with the rentamummy sign. The expense of an ad in the local paper (which you need a magnifying glass to read), 500 balloons and a mahoosive canister of helium gas has just about wiped me out financially, but I still need a sign to tell everyone what the stand is about. Poverty rather than necessity being the mother of invention, last night I set about making a sign at home using Boy One's art paper. (Top tip: lining paper from the DIY shop is about four quid for a million metres of thick painting paper. Just masking-tape it to the dining table and leave them to make a mess. You simply roll the whole thing up and bin it later – 'But it was too big to keep on the fridge, darling!') I also borrowed his blue, red and white poster paints, an art scalpel and some letters printed off the computer, then I set to work. *Blue Peter* would have been proud.

Mixing the paint to just the right shade of rentamummy lilac, I cut out stencils in the rentamummy font and lined them up along the lining paper across the living-room floor. On my hands and knees at 11 pm, I ever-so-carefully painted in the letters while shouting at and thumping the Husband on the legs every time he so much as looked like standing on my handiwork. Left to dry overnight it looked pretty professional from a distance. From close up it looked like a ten-year-old's art project, but I figured that by the time people realised what a 'sticky-back plastic' outfit rentamummy was they'd be too close to the stall to back out.

Now, as I wrestle the sign up to one end of the gazebo, I realise I really could do with an extra pair of hands. I'm buggered if I'm going to ask the squaddies who are already circling round the front of the stand muttering, 'renta-mummy!' and sniggering. Squaddies don't have 'mummies'. The posh ones have a 'mater' and the infantry have a 'mam' and neither is anything as soft as needing his mummy. I make a mental note to make both my boys marshmallow soft so that they always call me Mummy and need me to bits. Is it too soon to teach them to knit?

With a mixture of extreme care and lots of luck, the 13 ft sign goes up without a hitch. So, it's a bit squint and off-centre, but who cares? It's up. There is a prize for the best turned-out stand at the show and I'm aware that renta-mummy won't make it within a country mile so I'm not even going to try. The stand is just a base to get talking – my real killer marketing technique is literally full of hot air. It is time to bring out the balloons.

All those years of working on a marketing magazine haven't been in vain. I've gleaned a few top tips in my time. For example: fliers immediately go out with the recycling or, if you're lucky, get used for writing shopping lists. They rarely ever get read, and almost never get kept. Trying to hand them out is practically an invitation to get punched half the time. Fliers are a necessary evil and people hate them, but they expect them. Mind you, there is a really good back-up plan for events like this. Balloons are snapped up greedily by parents trying to defer junior's tantrum for just half an hour longer. Balloons work even if the business has nothing to do with children. Just print up a few hundred balloons with your logo, or even better your website address and let the children do the work for you. Why?

1. Because you give the balloon to the kiddie, they are then super-ultra-mega-happy. They decide they love you.
2. Mum and Dad are also happy because a) it keeps kiddie happy and therefore out of their hair, and b) it is free. They also decide they love you.
3. The balloon stays inflated and hangs around at home for days, gradually insinuating your company name into Mum and Dad's brain until they can't help but remember it.
4. No one can resist a balloon.

Having conveniently dropped his mobile phone into a vat of 80 per cent hydrochloric acid (there's a challenge for Motorola – call your phones rugged? Hah!) the Husband wandered off into the general melee and has been gone for what seems like hours now. As I don't possess a watch I don't know exactly how long he's been gone, only that it feels like hours and that's the important thing. Looking at the sun, and more accurately at the burgers most show-goers are carrying, it seems to be roughly lunchtime. My fingers are numb from tying knots in balloon ends, my back is aching from bending over a helium canister and my grin has already become fixed. I think my earlobes are cramping.

Spying the Husband weaving back through the crowd, I'm all ready with a touch of gentle nagging – it's a little early for full-bore bickering, but there's time – until I notice that he's bearing a cool pint of bitter in each hand. I could almost kiss him. He touches down for a brief second, scooping up Boy One who has been driving me absolutely mad for the last God knows how long (again, no watch but it feels like ...), and before I know it he's off into the masses once again.

The pint, however, remains and I pounce on it as if I haven't seen liquid for days. Having run out of the house at 7 am with a croissant stuffed in my mouth and my trousers barely done up, I realise that I haven't, in fact, drunk anything since 8 pm last night. This pint is very welcome. I tip my head back and delight in fizzy coldness, but then it slowly dawns on me where and who I am. I am rentamummy. That is, the woman to whom you trust your most precious possession – your children. I am a responsible adult, always in charge of her faculties, ready to act in an emergency and always setting a good example. Like Mary Poppins, but unlikely to use an umbrella as a legitimate mode of transport. And I am standing at the front of a trade stall advertising this to all the families in the area. All my potential clients are walking back and forth in front of this stall looking at me, checking me out. And right now they're watching me greedily necking a pint of bitter as if my life depended on it. Though it feels late I'm still not entirely sure whether it's suitably past the weekend lunchtime drinking hour. For all I know I could be boozing away at 10.30 am in a tent filled with four-year-olds and babies.

Slowly – and very reluctantly – I take the pint away from my lips and tuck it discreetly behind the back leg of the gazebo. Next quiet bit I get I'll sneak behind the squaddies' tent and have a good gulp. I'll worry about what to do with the beery breath afterwards.

But as I return to my post I realise that beer is the only liquid refreshment the Husband brought back with him. I barely managed a little sip of it before secreting it in its hiding place so I'm still dying of thirst. At least I'll have no problem smiling at potential clients. I'm so dehydrated that my lips are glued to my teeth in a lovely toothy grin.

Booze: 1; Paragon of Motherly Virtue: 0

The stall all set up and ready to go, we set about blowing up more balloons while waiting for customers. As time ticks by there seem to be few children wanting to be transformed into butterflies or tigers by my face painter who is sitting forlornly on one of the chairs she 'borrowed' from the nursery. The ground is still a bit soggy so she's also gradually sinking into the sod. I wonder if she's thinking that this was a good way to spend her Saturday? After a quick tour of the stalls, my face painter's mother returns with some bad news. An estate agent on a stall round the corner – and, crucially, placed right on the main drag – is offering face painting for a token donation (I know things are bad for estate agents in the credit crunch – I didn't realise they are relying on charity now, for heaven's sake). Are they stealing all our paying customers?

Balloon production is stepped up as I decide the only way to pull in the punters is to tour the show handing out freebies. Once we are sure that carrying 40 helium balloons is unlikely to make me take off into the skies, I set off to drum up some business. Halfway round and I am doing a great trade in free balloons and only slightly forced bonhomie. But then I realise a fatal flaw in my plan. If I am here drumming up business for the face painter and, by extension, rentamummy, there is no one manning the stall to talk up the business. The face painter is no doubt racking up the money as I drive five-year-olds and their parents her way, but I'm not there to take advantage of the captive audience.

I dole out the rest of the balloons with indecent haste. The 15-year-old on whom I foist my last balloon isn't convinced that rentamummy's lilac logo is doing his street cred any good whatsoever. I arrive back at the stall to see a family of four melt back into the crowd and the face painter happily pocketing six quid for her troubles. The balloon fairy is going to have to ply her trade much closer to home for the time being.

Unable to actually sell anything and with little to demonstrate, rentamummy's stall looks a little bare in comparison to the brightly decked tepee sellers, book stalls and llama farm. Families walk by and ogle, obviously intrigued as to what the hell rentamummy is, but they are too cautious to stick their necks out and visit the friendless lady hovering beside her spatulas. (In what passes for marketing shorthand, I'd decided that a small vase with two pastel spatulas and a wooden spoon will 'communicate' mummy-ness to passers-by.) The irony is that people complain about not getting one-to-one service, but hate being the only punter around.

I am therefore indecently happy to see the Partner in Crime hove into view from behind a tasty-looking bullock, extended family in tow. I practically drag her to the stand, instructing her and her sister, Brave Mother of Twins, to have a rest, take a load off, sit for a while. Never mind that they have just arrived at the show and are full of energy, raring to go. But, bless their kind hearts, they stay for a while doing such rentamummy-ish things as changing nappies, engaging in arts and crafts and generally looking happy to be there. The magic works and soon people begin making their way to the stand, comforted by the domestic scene playing out before them.

Soon, a steady stream of curious parents is wandering to and fro on the stand. Some even stay to paint the plaster of Paris snails that I've been painstakingly moulding for the last month. Most take a balloon and show a passing interest in the service before going on their way, dragging truculent four-year-olds in their wake: 'But I want to be a zebraaaaaaa!'

No one has yet taken up the offer of the breastfeeding station, which is hardly surprising considering the number of squaddies beaming at us from next door, but one mother does take up the offer of somewhere slightly less muddy than average to change her son's nappy. The Husband even returns from his wanderings with a venison burger. (I have one criticism of agricultural shows in general. I know that they're very pragmatic about this whole circle of life/foodchain issue. And I know that so-called dumb animals can't read. But it is a tad insensitive to park the burger van between the cow and deer pens. I'm not sure they enjoy sniffing Great Uncle George being sizzled to a turn as they graze nearby.) All in all things are looking up.

The Husband is about to set some lemonade and my burger down on the rentamummy trestle table when I squeal, possibly louder than necessary, 'STOP!' I point out three times in all that one end of the table is held up by little more than a ribbon and enormous good fortune. Dumping several hundred ounces of Bambi burger and half a pint of 7Up might be just enough to send the whole lot crashing down. This does not inspire confidence in the baby-changing woman who at that point has stationed her baby under the rickety end of the table. Setting a wipe-n-swipe world record, she has her son's dungarees up in seconds and begins edging away from the rentamummy death trap.

Booze, Health and Safety: 2; Paragon of Motherly Virtue: 0.

As lunchtime progresses, the show fills up and passing trade grows heavier. More and more people come to the stall and stop to be turned into lions. One My Little Pony looks rather more like My Little Purple Cat but the little girl is happy with the overall result so who can complain. It is also becoming abundantly clear that the charity-case estate agent round the corner is paying charity rates to his face painter and the result can be graded accordingly. His Dalmatian appears to be a totally white face with a black eye, and a lion seems to be simply a yellow face. My face painter is doing a fairly hot trade.

Among the people I am collaring the response is overall quite positive. I grow bolder and start tackling people before they come over of their own accord. This being the shires, there are the inevitable few who reply: 'Erw, new tharnks. We hev a ninny.' I am ready for them, though: 'Ah, but what happens if your ninny – sorry, nanny – is sick?' Admittedly some have a comeback for that too: 'Erw, then the other ninny takes both Felix *and* Araminta.'

Though today is primarily about rentamummy, I did bring some of the doula leaflets too. I consider accosting pregnant women as they go past but think better of it. You don't go for a day out to be chased by some woman offering to monitor your flappy bits.

One of the betweeded country gents is having a look over the stall and I am gearing up for the 'ninny' conversation, when he surprises me somewhat.

'You're a doula, are you? I've always thought they were a great idea.'

'Um, yes I am. Are you expecting? Or rather, is your wife?'

'No, not us, but we have a friend who's just had a baby and is in a bit of a state. Do you just do births, or do you do afterwards too?'

'Oh, both – I do both. Do you think your friend would like a postnatal doula?'

I'm so shocked by his interest I think I jabber a bit and I may be acting a little too keen, in a possibly scary *Hand that Rocks the Cradle* kind of way. But if Mr Tweed notices, he doesn't show it.

'I think she really could do with your help. Do you cover my area?'

I don't think Mr Tweed realises that I'm so grateful for his interest that even if his area were the Outer Hebrides I'd still cover it. We finish our brief chat and he leaves with doula and rentamummy leaflets, promising to have a word with his friend and get back to me as soon as possible. I'm so chuffed to be making progress that I punch the air and do a little jig on the spot. Unfortunately I stand on a balloon that then bursts, setting Boy Two screaming and making the face painter jump out of her skin. To give her her due, she seamlessly integrates the slash of black paint she's just drawn across a six-year-old's face into the pirate design she's about to finish. Another happy customer.

As the afternoon winds on, trade seems to slow a little. I decide it's time to renew the marketing campaign and prepare another balloon run. I'm bent double over the helium canister again, with the valve making unholy farting noises and my arse pointing to the sky. Suddenly I hear:

'rentamummy! We've been looking for you all day.'

For a minute I assume they must have been touring around all day looking for a woman with a big bum and now that mine is pointing to the sky they think they've found her.

(Not that I have a big bum. It's the only thing about me that isn't big. In fact, it's disappointingly small. I've often thought that this dieting lark would be much easier – and fairer – if it were possible to relocate bits of fat around the body. My stubborn joey pouch, for example, would look very J-Lo parked on my rump rather than on my tum, where it's very Ann Widdecombe. My tum would then be flat and I could happily continue inflating my glutes with chocolate instead of feeding joey rice cakes. But I digress …)

Eventually I realise that as I am bending down people can read my sign in full for a change and this is how they know that I am rentamummy. Straightening up I am presented with the epitome of the country mumkin:

expensively highlighted hair, country staples of gilet, jeans and jumper (rendered body-con tight with Lycra and cotton jersey instead of tweed and wool), designer sunglasses, Bugaboo pushchair and child by Mini Boden. Three of them. All no doubt struggling to squeeze their post-baby bodies into size 4 instead of a heiferish size 8.

'We've read all about you in the *Standard* and we wanted to come and find out about you.'

This sort of comment does the ego no damage at all. I launch into my spiel about the ninny being off sick (I long ago abandoned saying when the childminder is sick – the mumkins of this manor don't use childminders, it's live-in or nothing), the lunch that's too, too darling to miss (mumkins don't have to do shopping for anything other than pleasure and certainly don't have business meetings – that's what marrying a hedge funder is for), or the crucial appointment (as likely to be a filling for worry lines as teeth). I pause for breath expecting the usual 'What a good idea!' followed by pocketing a leaflet and trundling off into the sunset.

But these ladies have read up, which is my fault seeing as I already put all the info in the ad I ran in the local paper yesterday. Now, they have questions:

'Are you insured?' says one.

'What about a criminal record check?' says another.

'Double, double toil and trouble …' says the third.

Actually, she asks if the rentamummies bring their own children to babysit but she may as well have started quoting

Macbeth because I wasn't really prepared for the inquisition that had just started.

'How many mums do you have in the area?' the second asks.

'Are Ofsted involved?' the first joins in.

'Do you have maximum numbers?' continues the third.

Even though I'd considered these questions I hadn't really done anything about them. 'It's just babysitting,' I'd told myself, 'no one's going to ask for that sort of thing.' I'd convinced myself that people would be happy with a basic service to begin with. After all, I was helping them out of a hole. I hadn't really considered what to do if people did want this kind of assurance. As part of the doula training we'd been encouraged to get Public Liability Insurance. For the most part it would come in handy if we boil-washed someone's cashmere Babygro, or spilled coffee on the white rug. It could be used for far more serious incidents regarding the baby or mother's safety but, like the elephant in the room, such worrying examples were quickly ignored. However, if you're insured, the peace of mind is there.

But with rentamummy's business model, insurance doesn't really work. All the mummies are effectively self-employed, having to deal with their own tax, national insurance, etc., and all out of £8 an hour. Until the business really takes off (fingers crossed) that £8 an hour is hardly going to be a regular, and therefore large, income. To ask them each to shell out about fifty quid on insuring themselves before they even have any gigs is a bit much. Does this mean that I'll have to go to every appointment that overtly asks for proof of insurance?

The three women – I'm fighting hard not to call them the Weird Sisters – bring all these questions back to the front and rock my confidence a little. I manage to fudge my way through all their questions (How many mums do you have in the area? Ooh about ten or so. Real answer: Two, if both my friends happen to be free – and so on). And now that I've done this big marketing push there is a very real possibility that in the next few days I'll have to make good on promises made as people begin to call in rentamummy for honest-to-goodness work.

Caught up in all the excitement of designing ads, creating fliers, the madness of ordering 500 latex balloons on a whim and standing in a muddy field in the home counties on a sunny autumn day, now is the first time the reality of it all hits home. Can I cope? Have I really thought this through? Will it work? Is this what I want?

Before I can thoroughly frighten myself, the Husband returns from one of his many sorties, this time proffering ice cream and a spectacularly muddy baby. Boy Two's entire lower half is brown sludge and a kaleidoscope of stains cover his once-white top. Hatless in the beating sunshine and sockless in the wet ground, here is yet another glowing recommendation of rentamummy to the larger populace. Fortunately, this being a farming community, albeit largely of the gentleman variety, most older women walking past delight in the sight of a properly grubby child. Mind you,

you can see those of the Weird Sisters' generation secretly reaching for the Milton Wipes.

Booze, Health and Safety, Public Health: 3; Paragon of Motherly Virtue: 0.

As the sun begins to slide behind the trees there are few visitors to the stand. Even the face painter's constant stream of customers slows to barely a trickle. We are on the home stretch and I can finally stop blowing up those sodding balloons. Slumped in an unused breastfeeding chair I examine the box of flaccid latex and question the wisdom of buying 500 of the damn things. Despite almost constant blowing and tying while I wasn't explaining the rentamummy concept for the umpteenth time, there still appears to be well over half the box left. I also have over half a tank of helium left – a fact hidden from the Husband who would cheerfully spend the rest of the evening singing like Alvin and the Chipmunks until his brain shrivels from lack of oxygen.

Even the tireless enthusiasm of the squaddies next door has waned and they begin to pack up their netting and jerry cans. We take that as our cue that enough is enough and I relieve the face painter from duty, sending her jangling off into the evening sunshine. She has an evening out with friends booked after the show and judging by the bulge in her handbag she has more than enough beer tokens to see the night through. Personally, I don't see how she has the energy to contemplate going out to paint the town red, but then she is 27 with no children or husband to prematurely age her.

As Boy Two squelches yet more bits of mud (I am sincerely hoping it is mud but, being a sheep pasture until three days ago …) between his stubby fingers, thankfully resisting the seven-month-old's urge to eat it, the Husband and I wrestle the gazebo to the ground. The hand-painted sign is ceremoniously taken down – and thrown away; unpainted snails are saved for another day and unclaimed painted ones go to join their live brothers and sisters in the rubbish bin. After about 20 minutes of feverish activity there is barely a trace that rentamummy had ever been there.

One of our stall neighbours, to whom we have barely nodded hello all day long, pops over just as we are putting the last of the detritus in the car.

'I don't suppose you're missing a small boy?' she says.

'WHAT!'

'Only, this one has been wandering around the parade ring shouting, "Mummy!" for the last five minutes and we think he might be yours.'

'Oh Christ … thanks!'

I want to eat my own head with embarrassment. We have only lost Boy One once before and that was for five minutes in a shopping mall. We'd turned to pay for a toy car and turned back to realise he had vanished. Cue a panicked run up and down the other units in the mall screaming his name and me experiencing the worst five minutes of my life, feeling physically sick and dizzy with fear. I gathered more than a few 'crazy lady' looks on the way. Eventually he was found playing happily in the information booth with unpaid-for Disney store merchandise. A kindly couple had seen him outside the store looking bewildered, as most two-year-olds do, and had whisked him off to Lost Kids.

I still get cold sweats when I think about taking him into a busy department store. I can hardly bear to let the Husband take him on a trip to London with its myriad lost-child possibilities. Last time he went to Legoland I was so beside myself with fear that I took a permanent marker and wrote the Husband's mobile number up the inside of both Boy One's arms. No flimsy wrist bands that could fall off for me. It took a fortnight before the number washed off.

And this time, without a care in the world, we let him wander off into a field of around 1,600 people AND WE DIDN'T EVEN MISS HIM. Repeat after me: Bad Mother, Bad Mother, Bad Mother.

Booze, Health and Safety, Public Health, Child Protection Services: 4; Paragon of Motherly Virtue: 0.

Climbing exhausted and muddy into the car we begin to make for home, via the gin shop. It has been a busy day – rentamummy turns out to be far more popular than I could have hoped, which is a cheering thought. I can't help but play the Weird Sisters' questions in the back of my mind, though. Have I really thought this through, or am I back at six years old again, playing shops with paper money and Mum's high heels? Shall I just quit while I'm ahead (or at least only about 500 quid in debt) and go back to my job, leave running a business to proper people with MBAs and things?

From the back seat a small voice pipes up:

'Daddy took me to lots of things today, Mummy. We had pink fluff and saw a bollock and the man showed me the cow's boobies. It had four boobies. You don't have four boobies, you only have two and they're for babies. I don't like your boobie milk 'cos I'm a big boy. But I do like you, Mummy. I love you.'

Booze, Health and Safety, Public Health, Child Protection Services: 4; Being a mummy, renta or otherwise: priceless.

Chapter 9

Baby Steps

Sunday 14 September 2008

Slump on the sofa, exhausted after the Big Show. The benefit of having been run off my feet yesterday is that today I can quite confidently sit back and wait for rentamummy's customers to come flooding in.

I am waiting for the phone to ring, any moment. Any. Moment. Now.

Monday 15 September 2008

Phone still hasn't rung. Visit rentamummy.com to check for broken links and send two or three test emails to info@rentamummy.com just in case something's gone wrong. I get distracted by Boy Two making a bid for freedom down the kitchen stairs.

He is now in possession of a shiny new egg on his forehead. Maybe we won't tell potential clients about the 'throwing kids down the stairs' habit. Once the screaming subsides to sobbing and that diminishes to a faint 'uh-uh-uh' when he seems to be gulping great teary breaths, I turn back to the computer with him balanced on my knee.

Hooray! On pulling up the site again I see the visitor counter has gone up a few *and* my inbox shows three new messages. I get as far as clicking 'Open' before realising that the emails are me testing the system (it works: good; there's no one using it: bad). The visitor counter is also showing every time I've checked the home page. There are 200 pesky kids with slowly deflating rentamummy balloons in their living rooms that their mothers have obviously failed to glance at even just once. Curses.

Tuesday 16 September 2008

The Glamazon has invited a gaggle of us pre-school mums (Are we a gaggle? A packed lunch of mums? A home corner? A gossip?) to celebrate her birthday at the local Indian restaurant. I feel a certain loyalty to this place as they have a habit of delivering a single red rose with every takeaway. Never mind that they do this regardless of whether the household consists of a just-engaged couple in the first flush of love, or a flatshare of staunchly heterosexual rugby players. I calculate that our curry house has bought me at least four times more flowers than the Husband. I hear that hot spices can make you amorous but that is ridiculous.

Naturally, the Husband is late, so the kids' supper is late, so my shower is late, so I am late. I enter the restaurant to scenes of feverish excitement. You can practically smell the hormones. Eyes are wide, cheeks are flushed and the table vibrates with hushed whispers of: 'He's here!', 'It's really him!', 'Go on, you go!' and '*I* wanted to stand next to him in the picture!'

Seeing that I'm somewhat bemused at missing out on an event of some obvious importance, the mum on my left leans over as if about to impart some earth-shattering news:

'He was here and we all had our picture taken with him and he's dead nice and he agreed to come up to the pre-school and I didn't realise but he *lives* here and he's really nice – I said that I didn't – anyway he is – and he's having a take-away and he's going soon and I'm going to show everyone my picture.'

Just as I begin to wonder if she has gills, she stops for a breath. Who could it be, I muse? They've been filming the new *James Bond* hereabouts and it would be rather nice to bump into him.

'Who was it?' I ask.

'MR TUMBLE OFF CBEEBIES!!' she reveals.

You can almost hear the *Pfeeeeeeeee* as my excitement deflates. It's saying something when you can suffer an oestrogen overdose at the sight of a children's TV presenter who regularly paints his nose red and wears size 40 multicoloured trousers, whose key demographic can be stopped in its tracks by a particularly fruitful digital exploration of the left nostril.

Suspecting that my tales of yonder years spent with R 'n' B stars showing off their 'piece' at after-show parties might be a little ... spicy for their taste, I begin to dread what the rest of the evening holds.

I can be a cynical old bat at times. Just because I think flouncing around London nightclubs watching the rich, famous and clueless at play is the bee's pyjamas, it doesn't mean that it's any more thrilling than a kids' entertainer on channel 405.

The rest of Glamazon's party is in fact perfectly pleasant. Actually it is bloody good fun. I spent so long living vicariously off my old life that perhaps I've failed to start enjoying the new one. I may temporarily be a Stay At Home Mum, I don't have to turn my brain to soup or find the prospect of a new tea towel just too, too exciting.

Equally, it's quite good fun to find out who's doing what to whom in the village, or get into a lather about the stupid council and its stupid plans for so-called 'early years education provision' (i.e. get in the queue early or there won't be any left).

The Glamazon is parked at the far end of the table so we don't get much chance to catch up about the idea that she and I might like to buddy up on the doula thing, but she introduces me to the sweetest Anzac mum who, somewhat amazingly, is walking and talking despite having given birth to her first child barely three weeks ago.

Still filled with the excitement and adrenaline of the new mum, she admits that the sleepless nights are getting to her a little bit. Fuelled by the bonhomie of a bunch of mums on the run, and possibly a glass or six of Pinot Grigio, I offer to take her daughter out for a walk or something, just to give Anzac Mum a chance for some guilt-free snooze.

Until you have children you don't realise what a precious commodity sleep is. You tell yourself that you pulled all-nighters before, at university or at parties when you'd happily go from Friday morning to Sunday lunchtime with nary a nap. What you don't realise is that spending the daylight hours semi-comatose, drinking coffee and shooting the breeze with your mates to help you recover, isn't an option when Boy One is refusing his third home-cooked meal of the day and Boy Two would like bosoms and nappy changes in strict rotation for the next four hours on the trot, if you please.

New mothers therefore don't want bottles of champagne (you can't drink it if you're breastfeeding anyway as it gives the baby wind – well, more wind than usual), designer clothes, pretty bassinets, baby baths (you really can bath a baby in the kitchen sink) or diamonds (actually that's a lie – we really, *really* do want diamonds). All they want is two hours of uninterrupted sleep.

I can't bring myself to offer Anzac Mum her two hours off at a price. We've only just met, she's Glamazon's friend, she's a great laugh, and I'm a total wimp when it comes to charging for things. This may prove to be a problem in the long run. We set a date and I decide that the look of relief that crosses her face is payment enough for now.

I must be getting into a giving mood because the chair-woman of the pre-school committee nobbles me in the middle of my sag aloo. I've been asked to be on the committee before and steadfastly refused. I know it's not because I'm just so fabulous, it's because they're utterly desperate and have about three people running the whole shooting match. This came as something of a surprise to me.

Rather stupidly, I thought that when the Government offered five half-day sessions to all parents of three-year-old children, they would actually pay for people to run them. But of course not. Instead, the Government throws a few shekels our way, which covers sticky-back plastic (which I took until my twenties to discover was Sellotape) and sand for the sand-pit. The rest we have to fund ourselves, which means more sponsored bounces, bulk-baking and dubious merchandise. Then you draft in all the mums (I would be equal opportunities and say dads too but we just know this isn't the case) to fill unimportant posts such as treasurer, fund-raiser, teaching assistant and so on. Cheap at none of the price.

I always refuse to be on these committees, not because I don't want to help – well, actually, I don't much – but because I am useless at them. I am unreliable, I over promise and under deliver, I'm lazy, I'm late and I'm generally a bit of a liability. But still they ask.

So during dinner I find myself running through ideas to make money for our new pre-school building. Merging my two main careers from the past of PR and marketing, we come up with suggestions of who to target, how and when. We even turn Mr Tumble into a promotional plan. Before I know it, I've been co-opted into running the PR for fund-raising activity for the new building. As I have so far been relatively unsuccessful in fund-raising for my own business, and by extension for my own salary, it seems a little foolish to promise the time to do it for others for free. Perhaps I'll get lucky and be so crap at it they'll fire me.

Wednesday 17 September 2008

Time for me to go out for a trot with Anzac's daughter. If anything it'll be good exercise for me as I have singularly failed to darken the doors of the gym for the last month and a half. It will also be a good dry run for the postnatal doula service. It'll give me an idea of what I can and can't achieve in two hours and how difficult it's going to be to run with Boy Two in tow. Up to now I'd blithely assumed that Boy Two could be offloaded on to the Very Capable Childminder when I got a job but she's now chocka with babies and there's no space at the inn. This means that on this occasion at least, baby comes too.

I put on my best 'you will look fantastic when your daughter is eight months old and be capable of all sorts of things as life returns to normal' face and head off. It is better than my real face, which is 'I haven't had more than two hours' consecutive sleep since October 2007 and my nipples are dropping off.' Like the ghost of motherhood future, I fear this may be rather frightening and it's not as if she can insure against it by buying the biggest turkey in the shop.

It's also been a while (seven months and one week precisely) since I cared for a three-week-old baby. Seeing as they'll make up the majority of my clients, it'll be good hands-on practice. I hope Anzac Mum doesn't mind a little child experimentation.

For a woman with a brand-new baby, Anzac Mum is surprisingly together. Yes, she's still in her pyjamas but I'm often to be found pottering around in PJs at all hours. In fact, the home-working wardrobe sometimes gets so bad that I have to create an antidote and get dressed up to the nines just to go to the supermarket.

I creep over to the carrycot and peep in at the *tiniest* little scrap. Anzac Mum swears she's 8 lbs at least but to me, with my 22 lb lump on my hip, she looks like a little doll. I'm almost afraid to pick her up in case I break her. Playing for time with a little cooing, oohing and aahing I give myself a stern talking-to that I can't be seen going all to bits in front of the woman. She's relying on me to look after her bub after all. Putting on what I think is my best 'bustling busybody' behaviour I scoop up nappies, wipes, dummies et al., hook my own infant onto my front in a sling and gather up the teeny one to be clicked into her pram frame. Mum is under strict instructions to go to bed and stay there until I get back in two hours. A cheery wave and I'm gone.

Rounding the corner and out of sight I come to a huffing,

puffing halt. I haven't used the front sling in weeks and it's clear that Boy Two has been verily enjoying all the pies since then. My back is aching and I still have to push the pram and carry this one all the way into the village. I'd breezily claimed that I was going to do a spot of shopping and have a nice wander around. At this rate I'll be lucky if I can crawl back to my house without crushing several vertebrae. I can't go back and get the car because I've just binned my baby car seat so have no way of getting the baby in. And I can't wake Anzac Mum up, especially since I claimed that this was a mere trifle to do.

On I slog, puffing up a hill I never noticed was there before. I arrive home and plop the baby into a rocker and dump Boy Two on the floor. He gives me a most quizzical look as if to say: 'Eight months and you replace me already, Mother? You have the attention span of a goldfish.' The next hour is a blur of soothing a rejected baby (mine), changing a dirty one (hers) and trying to figure out how to get back to Anzac Mum's without bursting something.

Crawling back we arrive just as she emerges from the shower. It was hard work but the change in the woman is most gratifying. It's amazing what an hour or so's kip can do for you. I wonder what would happen to the beauty industry and its hundred-quid creams if the secret got out that you can look a damn sight better if your husband and kids would just leave you in peace once in a while. Probably implode over night.

I follow my intensely physical first doula-ing experience with Tumble Tots for Boy Two, the weekly shop and collecting

Boy One from the Very Capable Childminder. By 7 pm I am a shadow of my former self and completely poleaxed.

To make the doula service a going concern I'm probably going to have to have two clients a day, at least three days a week. I'm also going to have to look after Boy Two for the foreseeable because even if there was space for him at the childminder's I couldn't afford it right now anyway. This basically means that by the end of the first week I could quite reasonably be dead.

Glamazon's birthday party comes back to bite me. Having waxed lyrical about what you could and couldn't do to promote the pre-school's fund-raising activities, an email is waiting in my inbox from the chair of the council's children's service. The chair of the pre-school committee has taken me at my word for the offer of help and given my details to this woman. That's fine, but from her message it looks like she thinks I'm a whole lot more enthusiastic than I am.

Subject: PUBLICITY

Thanks for your offer to DO Publicity for the Project. That is great news.

We need asap: (1) an item on Radio Berkshire – and I am very willing to talk about the Project – if appropriate. (What time is your slot – and where?) Possibly followed by short updates on progress for the next 12 months – we hope the pre-school will open in the new building next Sept.

(2) a design for a leaflet to drop in all the houses on the estates, to inform them of the Project and ask for ££ support. We are not going to do a noisy follow-up House to House collection, unfortunately – BUT we can ask families who have been involved with the school in the past 30+ years –

i) to support our Fund-raising for new equipment for the new building – and send cash, cheques to be handed in to ... tbc. (If we can add an envelope to the leaflet, I will take on knocking on selected doors. Tbc)

ii) to tell us the stories of previous pre-schoolers, and what they have done since they left.

iii) We anticipate creating a world map – to record where previous school children now live as adults ...

That last may be something someone else wants to take on – but publicising it would be the first step.

Hope that puts you in the picture. Do phone me back when convenient.

Oh shit.

Thursday 18 September 2008

Hallelujah! My inbox is bursting with mail, stuffed even. And only a few of them are Nigerians telling me that I'm the ideal person to help them move this inconveniently large sum of money out of the country and would I mind keeping around £100k because this cheque is just too big for them to handle …

No, not bookings for rentamummy, that's just foolishness. I've had an email from a qualified nursery nurse, fully criminal checked and ready and raring to be one of our mummies. While this doesn't bring any money in directly, she's a more attractive person to put out there as a rentamummy than some of my friends. While absolutely the most decent and delightful people, their professional recommendation goes little further than 'being a good egg because our children play together'. Now I have to scrape together the terms and conditions pack that I've promised her and which I haven't updated, refined or in fact given a second glance to since I was last surprised like this.

However, and possibly more importantly, I have six fresh juicy RSVPs to Boy One's birthday party. The crisis of how many Party Bags to make up looks closer to being solved. I've been having sleepless nights about angelic faces looking up at me expectantly and not having any cake or bag to give them. Watching a little child's face crumple into tears just kills me. I've used my position in my regular radio slot to promote things before, but is it a bit weird to use a regional radio show to ask your son's pre-school friends to pull their fingers out and RSV-bloody-P?

At the moment I have other fish to fry. Excited though I am by the emails clogging my inbox, I have to get a wriggle on because we're leaving the house an hour earlier today. In their wisdom, the editorial team behind Henry K's show has decided that it's a bit inconvenient to have Producer Man looking after Boy Two rather than actually running the show. I mean, really! He's very manageable, only tries to chew through one or two wires, loves trying to put through the travel report and has even tried to join in presenting the show a couple of times by inadvertently gargling into the intercom. However, the team would rather he was childminded for the time I'm on air. This would be fine if they a) paid me, b) paid me, or c) paid me. But they don't. It's impossible to put him into proper childcare anyway, as they keep chopping and changing the day I'm on. Come on Auntie Beeb – sort it out!

Today I manage to put Boy One into his childminder an hour early (costing an extra £5 you realise), bundle Boy Two into the car and shoot off in the opposite direction to the radio station to deposit him with the Partner in Crime before driving back again (another £5 in diesel) to get on air on time. I try pointing out that it'll cost me a good £25 a week to get Boy Two looked after for the time they want me.

It's a particularly peculiar situation because I appear to have been 'promoted', if that's possible. I'm now supposed to get involved in interviewing callers to the station and whatnot.

It's all good fun but it doesn't resolve the problem that I'm paying for the pleasure. There is a suggestion that I may just be able to claim on expenses, but that idea is swiftly quashed. Apparently there's a common response inside the BBC to this sort of request:

'Blame Jonathan Ross.'

Later in the day I receive yet another rentamummy email and it intrigues me:

I am on the committee of the toddler group and we are currently looking for more retailers to come into the sessions and sell to parents. We typically have a lot of the franchises aimed at kids/parents (Usborne books, Phoenix cards, etc.) coming in, but are hoping to attract some new more original businesses, and after reading the piece about you in the local paper I think your service could be of interest to our members.

We provide a designated area and tables for you (near the teas/coffees) and have at least 25 parents attending each session. As we head towards Christmas and the weather gets worse, we get far busier. There is no charge for the pitch, but we ask for 10 per cent of anything you make on the product (which we then use as a prize for our Xmas raffle, which then goes towards rent and new toys, etc.).

It all looks like a good opportunity to promote the service but I have just one question: how do I give away 10 per cent of a rentamummy? Chop off her fingers?

Admittedly I could give away 10 per cent of the booking fees and whatnot, but as this currently stands at £0.00, it wouldn't buy the most sought-after prize in the raffle. However, it might not be a bad idea to contribute two hours of rentamummy babysitting as a prize in the Christmas raffle itself, so that parents can skip out for a cheeky gluwein or two. But it does mean that I'll have to a) pay the rentamummy myself, or b) look after the little darlings myself. I think I prefer a).

Saturday 20 September 2008

This inbox of mine is really coming up trumps lately. A mum tripped over the rentamummy.com website today and claims that she's going to sign herself and her friend up! Hooray! A bit 'Boo' that she doesn't want to use a rentamummy right now, of course, but slowly, slowly catchee monkey as they (whoever 'they' are) say.

It also turns out that she is part of another mumpreneur business making ready meals for kids that's been going for a while now and is a pretty good little earner by all accounts. Waitrose, that great supporter of local goods (or at least it claims to be) is a real hotbed of mum-made meals. In fact, it was something I'd considered many moons ago myself, but the thought of public health inspectors checking every nook and cranny of my kitchen gives me the willies. Frankly, if they saw my kitchen it would give them the willies too. To be honest I've always found these ready meals a bit pricey but I suppose that because I'm a Stay At Home Mum with nothing to do all day but play wind the bobbin up (snort). I have more than enough time to mash a potato and boil some spaghetti. Besides, as Boy One has remained on his fussy eating fad for nearly six months, I'm loath to spend nearly three quid on something he'll spit out, when I can make something that he'll spit out for 50p instead.

Foodie Mum wants to know if they could do some kind of promotional tie-in with rentamummy, perhaps offering discount coupons to the first five people in the month who book with us. I refrain from telling her that at the moment we need every incentive we can find to get mums to use us.

Sunday 21 September 2008

Celeb Mum comes to the local market town for their annual literary festival. I bought tickets ages ago and sent a message saying we should maybe meet up and have a chat afterwards, compare notes on the book front. Although the note-comparing will hardly be equal. Since I last saw her she has trotted out another best-selling novel and become a bit of a poster girl for the posher end of the mother-working-from-home spectrum. Also, my last two messages have gone completely ignored so I'm quite worried that she might think I'm turn-ing into a stalker. Or, worse, that she thinks I have a 'pash' on her. It was definitely a thing in the 1980s that public-school girls could develop 'pashes' on older prefects. Not quite your full-blown lesbian crush, there was a certain amount of adula-tion and emulation of the older girl, which generally younger girls grew out of as soon as boys their own age ceased to resemble pizzas and discovered Axe deodorant.

Other Mother of Boys and I go to watch her discuss her books and soak up some gossipy titbits about the fast London set she runs with (the only thing you run with out here in the boondocks are dogs – canine or human, take your pick). I'm about to give in to my inner mouse and skulk out afterwards when I decide no, damn it, if she is avoiding me then I can at least accost her in public and find out for sure. I don't think she'll tell me to my face to sling my hook but I'll probably be able to tell from the 'fight or flight' look in her eyes.

As it is she neither fights nor flies, but pumps my hand with a very strong handshake and lets rip with a battery of questions: 'How *are* you? Ages since I saw you! Had to dump Facebook, y'know – too many odd people. Sorry not to be in touch. Business good?' I burble something about it doing really well, she duly gives me a good few lines of puff to put on the website and then I am bulldozed by a phalanx of 60-something women wanting signed copies.

Monday 22 September 2008

The Husband has the day off and volunteers to look after the children while I catch up with all the jobs that need doing following rentamummy's new-found popularity. To save him having to pound the pavements with a baby strapped to his front, I volunteer to hit the library with the laptop. It will also remove me from the fridge, which I have taken to visiting with alarming regularity.

The library has a pleasing 'university' feel about it, with those cubby-hole desks that are the furniture equivalent of putting your arm round your exercise book to stop classmates copying your work. I note that council facilities have yet to enter the twenty-first century and there is no such thing as Wi-Fi, but I can always use the library computers if I need to email.

I saunter up to the desk swinging my power cord and ask a librarian where I can plug myself in.

'You can't plug that in here,' she replies.

'Why on earth not?'

'You just can't. You can still use your laptop, of course.'

'But it only has two hours of battery life.'

'Then you can use the library computers – we have 20-minute slots.'

Shaking my head in disbelief I return to my cubby hole. It's like going back to the Dark Ages, or at least to 1998 when I worked in a PR agency and seven of us all shared the same 56k dial-up account. Every five minutes someone would shout across the office: 'Get off your webmail, Ali, I need to send a press release to the *Telegraph*.'

Losing myself in the intricacies of creating a proper renta-mummy Application Pack I notice some time later that my battery life is now critical. I need to find somewhere to plug myself in, and quickly.

I contemplate going back to the gym where I can have another go at trying to connect to their Wi-Fi but I haven't been for about six weeks and the personal trainer is bound to corner me and mentally size up the increase in my muffin top. But I can't stay here.

Mooching up the street I don't get very far before coming across a very attractive and, crucially, virtually empty pub that is offering its Wi-Fi free to customers. I tentatively enquire as to whether or not they might share some of their finest elec-tricity with me as well and they practically jump on me. Judging by the emptiness of the place I think they're quite desperate for customers.

Cosily installed next to the power point and wireless box I get stuck back in and the process is now made much more pleasant by being able to check my Facebook every now and again. That and the large glass of Pinot Grigio on the table. When I finally get up to leave, having achieved quite a lot of business admin, I'm a little embarrassed to settle my bill when I've been ensconced there for the best part of four hours. As office rentals go, £4.50 is quite reasonable.

Wednesday 24 September 2008

The Stepmonster arrives today to visit his Steprunts for the first time in their native environment. He's always seen them on visits to the venerable grandmother, when they've been on their best behaviour on pain of removal of chocolate privileges. Now he's on their territory he might be in for a shock.

Unfortunately, unlike the Outlaws, the Stepmonster has no innate childcare abilities. He took delivery of me when I was about eight years old so the whole nappies/tantrums/potty training debacle largely passed him by. The look on his face when he was asked to change a wet nappy a couple of years back was priceless.

This means that instead of a greater division of labour over the next few days, there's likely to be a multiplication of it, as he expects coffees, beers and a selection of cold meats to be brought forth. He also has an annoying habit of leaving small, chokeable items such as nuts, needles and coins lying around on the floor for the smalls to come along and munch. Workload and parental paranoia are about to double.

I take Anzac Mum's daughter for her weekly perambulate. This time I'm a bit better equipped, having dragged the back carrier out of the attic, so some of the strain from my poor old spine is removed. You can't get rid of it all, however, and I can feel that 22 lbs of boy is giving my thighs a good workout up and down the gentle village inclines. It certainly gives me an incentive not to put on any more weight if this is what really hefty people have to carry around with them all day.

Unfortunately the back carrier also specialises in holding Boy Two in a bit of a stranglehold so, crossing the humped railway bridge, I decide it's time for a bit of readjustment to stop the gentle lilac colour he's now sporting from turning to a deep royal blue. Putting the brakes on the baby's pram, I turn to fiddle with Boy Two's straps.

I don't know what makes me turn around, there is no horn or screeching tyres. But when I do glance back I see the baby's pram gently heading into the middle of the road where, miraculously, both lanes are empty – although not for long, as a blue transit rounds the corner and heads straight for her.

'SHIIIIIIIT!' I yell as I leap into the road and grab the gently circling pram, yanking it back onto the pavement. I don't even look behind me as I jump so theoretically I could have achieved the triple whammy of getting all three of us squashed in one go.

I have nearly killed someone else's baby.

If it sounds dramatic, that's how it feels.

In reality, the pram just bumped off the pavement, which is probably what made me turn around. That I barely had to pull it back up the kerb means that it wasn't actually coursing into oncoming motorway traffic. But however close a call it was, I cling on to that pram for dear life all the way to the supermarket.

Thursday 25 September 2008

The reason Stepmonster is here is to take part in the festivities for Boy One's fourth birthday. One of the great joys of being a parent is a birthday. Yes, if you're on a budget it can be a painfully expensive business, but nothing is going to beat the look on a small boy's face when he's confronted with a massive pile of shiny parcels and told to get stuck in. Today is party day and therefore a designated no-work day (apart from the usual siren call of Radio Berks, but that's more like gossiping than actual work). No emails will be checked. Paper plates will be arranged, balloons blown up, presents opened, fun had.

On the present front, I am eternally grateful to the gods of advertising. Both Partner in Crime and Other Mother of Boys think I am mad to let Boy One watch cartoons on commercial telly. Personally, I find some of the wholewheat versions of kiddies' entertainment you get on the licence-fee channels make me want to scream after a while. I'm in a much happier place confronted with Noddy or Rupert Bear.

I find the ads quite instructive, and not because years of working on a marketing magazine have brainwashed me. It gives you a good heads-up as to what little girls and boys are going to be into, so when you turn up at kids' parties you don't get the quizzical look of death when you proudly present the birthday child with an instructional video on origami.

Extensive research and many days spent listening to Boy

One as he points out that he wants 'that one … and that one … and that one …' mean that this year I think the Husband and I have got it spot on. One massive, mega, super-huge-mongous space shuttle and a vat of play sand lie in wait under acres of silver wrapping. After much crumpling, yikes-ing, yay-ing and rending asunder of boxes otherwise impenetrable to an adult, he clatters off downstairs to lose as many crucial pieces as possible by breakfast time.

But even though I'm looking forward to absorbing the party spirit vicariously via the four year old, the long list of tasks ahead doesn't make me spring from the bed with unalloyed joy. The Husband and I slowly peel ourselves out of bed and get ready for a day of sugar-fuelled children and mammoth bin bags. He repairs to the kitchen while I scrape what's left of our son off the ceiling and try to pour him into his clothes for a morning spent at the Very Capable Childminder. Then it happens.

Making a cup of coffee and doing toast with honey for Boy One in a clearly ill-advised attempt to multitask, the Husband misjudges the location of its base, and brings the kettle in too low for a landing. Its bottom half slices through the top two layers of my meticulously created volcano cake.

'Oops. Oh no. Oh. Um. Sorry.'

Very quietly the Husband calls me into the kitchen. There in front of me are the remains of three hours of baking, rolling and sticking. With barely five hours until the arrival of five adults, five children between two and four, and three babies,

I am faced with the completely destroyed remnants of Boy One's birthday cake.

There is a brief moment of silence.

Then I run upstairs, howling. When Boy One asks what's wrong some quick thinking comes up with 'I've stubbed my toe, darling.' Five minutes later, composed, but shaking with anger, I descend. The Husband looks genuinely terrified but I just get on with the day's usual demands – socks, lunch, breakfast things, throwing four tiers of black forest gateau with extra dinosaurs in the bin. The Husband goes to leave, distinctly downcast; at least he's sorry. But right now, sorry just isn't cutting it.

'When will you be back?' I ask, curtly.

'I don't think I should come back,' he replies.

Normally I'd take that as a throwaway comment, but it's said so deadpan I actually believe he may mean it. So, the bastard is going to wreck the birthday cake and leave me, all in the same day?

'Don't be bloody silly,' is the only answer I can think of.

'But you don't look like you want me to come back. You look like you hate me.'

'And right now I do, but that's no reason to leave. You have to come back later so I can punish and torture you.'

He leaves for his train, understandably nervous that I now have nine uninterrupted hours to think of innovative and horrible ways to get my own back.

Boy One's tea party isn't until four o'clock, which seems

like plenty of time to get everything going again, but with the
Stepmonster and an hour on the radio in the way it feels as if
there is hardly any time at all. I quickly knock up another
volcano cake (better than the first attempt I have to admit)
and head off for the station once more. Being on air proves
cathartic as I take the opportunity to relate the cake tale to the
rest of the county and invite callers' commiserations. By the
end, I hardly feel angry at all. Which is a shame.

Friday 21 September 2008

Not a phrase you hear often, granted, but I get in touch with
the Editrix as an interesting marketing nugget has come my
way and I thought I should pass it on. She replies with a
potted history of what's been going on with the magazine for
the last – ooh – six months. They've moved to new offices that
are brighter and nicer, which of course they would be while
I'm not there. The magazine has expanded, with a proper
number of staff, rather than being the string and sticky-tape
operation I left last year. She has even sent over an electronic
copy of the newly revamped magazine. It now has advertising
(people don't trust a magazine without advertising), which
makes it look really …

… good. Which is a worry.

It's a worry because it would have been quite easy not to
go back to a failing trade magazine with few subscribers and
even fewer profits. It would have been simple to hand in my

notice to an office that was obviously suffering from sick building syndrome, where plants and cockroaches go to die. But now it's not going to be easy at all.

The Partner in Crime is enjoying (though that's probably not the right word) her last day of maternity leave before going back to work on Monday. Like many new mums she's going back part time so she can still enjoy the so-called trappings of being a Stay At Home Mum, such as *Inspector Morse* marathons.

She's been going through hell trying to get her one-year-old to adapt to the nursery, regularly having to leave with his cries echoing in her ears. Odd that they should call it 'settling in'. It ought to be 'unsettling'.

But until now I have been thinking that I am lucky to be out of all that. I can choose the hours I work. I can choose to be at home with the kids, or go for a swim in the pool (bliss!) when I want to. There's no more cursing the trains because I'm late again. Or getting back well after dark because the tube station is once more closed due to overcrowding. (Whodathunk it? A lot of people want to use central London tube stations at rush hour. Shouldn't be allowed, should it? Oh, it isn't.)

But there are no more accidental shopping trips to Selfridges, promising to make up the hours at the end of the day. There are no more client lunches (unless you count baby smush and stimulating gurgling over a glass or two of Ribena), or ad agency parties that descend into debauchery with frightening speed. No more freebies. No more life?

The Stepmonster continues to clutter up the house, even though he's staying at a local B&B. It's like having a third (or, depending on the Husband's mood, fourth) child around. I pack two children into the car to deposit one at pre-school and then on to Stepmonster's accommodation to collect him. Thereafter demands for 'What are we doing today?' entertainments and lunches created, more taxiing around the county and back for more meals. The look of boredom on Stepmonster's face when confronted by the minutiae of daily life show that he probably had a lucky escape acquiring me when nearly fully formed, or at least capable of getting from A to B on my own. He's not really cut out to be a stay-at-home grandpa. Looks like The Outlaws will be getting called upon for a bit longer.

Sunday 28 September 2008

I'm going to meet my first bona fide doula client tomorrow and I'm actually quite nervous. She has a real problem that she needs real answers to and I suddenly have a crisis of confidence. What if I can't give her the information she needs? What if she thinks doulas are a waste of money?

I try to do some half-hearted preparation on the internet. As doulas we're not supposed to give advice but we can give information. The line is pretty fine and I'm quite sure I'm going to cross it. Plus, I'm quite sure that the problem she's told me about over email will turn out to be a completely different one when I turn up.

Nervous Mum wants me to think of ways to get her baby to sleep peacefully in her bassinet and be put down without crying. Perhaps I could find her the holy grail while I'm at it. I don't have the heart to tell her that I still rely on shoving a bosom into Boy Two to coax him to sleep and that for the last two weeks teething has meant that he gets up at least five times in the night. Since he learned to crawl he has also figured out how to roll over, crawl out of his cot and over my prone, snoring body, and position himself on my front ready to clamp down. This would be fine if he could achieve it all without waking me up but he uses my face to boost himself forward and latches on enthusiastically, forgetting about the newly sprouted top and bottom teeth. Routinely raw of nipple and fuzzy of brain, I suspect I may be getting even less sleep than my client.

As always, I'm caught completely on the hop. I haven't sorted out the public liability insurance (I am sure I am 100 per cent public liability), made sure my car insurance covers travelling to jobs, arranged my 'doula bag', looked into cover for Boy Two – it's all a bit of a mess.

But now is not the time to start having a wobbly. If I'm going to think like that I may as well tear up the resignation letter and get back on the tube.

Monday 29 September 2008

Shockingly, I get to the client's house early. I decide it's a bit weird to sit outside for ten minutes so that I'm officially 'between 7 pm and 8 pm', particularly as the Multipla is a diesel and rattlier than Keith Richards before his first fag of the morning.

We sit down in the living room and she looks like every other mother of a five-week-old baby. Knackered, in other words. We discuss the problem of the baby refusing to go down in her Moses basket in the evening and refusing to be quiet unless she's being cuddled or fed. I resist the temptation to say that this is pretty much par for the course for newborns and that her best tactic is to get used to it. After all, she's got me here for answers, not to confirm what I suspect she already knows. So I set about going through the possible solutions to her problem: swaddling, different bedtimes, white noise, sleeping bags, etc. She looks sceptical at first and not at all impressed when I warn her that she may have to try things over and over again before her daughter settles on something she likes.

In the end I think it all goes OK, but it'll be a tough job. I get the impression that she likes me and she seems keen to sort out some dates then and there. I give her the spiel: 'Don't worry if you don't want to go ahead, that's why I come on these chats – so you know exactly what you're getting and what you might want.' Then, driving away, I regret it. Have I just done myself out of a job?

Tuesday 30 September 2008

The credit crunch appears to be biting. In fact, credit crunch hardly seems appropriate as the economy is being crunched, chewed and spat out. President Bush seems to have lost all control – comes to something when the head of financial institutions has to actually get on his knees and beg another politician to pass a bill. Usually when politicians are on their knees they are engaged in something altogether more pleasant.

The upshot in our area is that there are a lot of people, men mainly, wandering around in a state of shock. Long lunches doing deals are evaporating. In many cases, whole jobs are evaporating altogether. Could this be bad news for rentamummy? After all, why would mums need a mummy to babysit their kids when a freshly unemployed banker is hanging around the house all day instead?

That said, when their daily contact with their children has been to have them presented at the dinner table, washed and scrubbed by nanny, with a fresh phrase in Mandarin practised and ready for word-perfect delivery, the ability to deal with them on a daily-grind-by-daily-grind basis will be limited. Besides, these men will take the opportunity to spend all day out on the golf course under the pretence of networking their way into a new job.

Even though the increasingly tabloid BBC would have us plunging headlong into a recession worse than the Great Depression of the 1930s, the Husband and I aren't too worried. For his part, he's fairly convinced that people will still (unfortunately; this isn't schadenfreude) get cancer and he will still be needed to try to cure it.

For my part, women will still get pregnant and still have babies, and despite the husbands being around more than usual they will continue to be a bit useless on the business end of a birth. Doulas are not yet an endangered species.

That said, today I am just waiting. From a flurry of emails back and forth before we met, the contact with my potential client has dried up. Has she had second thoughts? I do hope not. She pointed out when we were talking that, as she had got the contact from Anzac Mum, once word of mouth takes off that's it, you're beating them off with a stick. Oh well, even if she doesn't take me up on the job, hopefully she'll have a good word to pass on to other mums she knows. But, still, the money would be nice …

Chapter 10

All Grown Up

Wednesday, October 2008

While I wait for news from the Nervous Mum, I trot up the road to take Anzac Mum's baby for a walk again. These short excursions are good little brainstorming moments for me. I can't be distracted by whatever drivel schedulers see fit to put on the box during weekday mornings. Nor can Boy Two drive me up the wall looking for entertainment. Fair enough, he's strapped to my back and currently tearing chunks of hair from my head, but he's otherwise peaceful. Anzac Mum's baby is a dream, simply goggling up at me from her pram wondering who is this two-headed monster and what's it done with her lunch.

So I have time to think. I wonder if this rentamummy lark is going to make me any money at all, or whether I should just cut my losses. The fact that The Meeting with the Editrix is imminent is really focusing my mind. It's all very well vowing never to darken their doors again but that was easily said when even the measly maternity pay was dripping into my bank account. Now that even that has stopped there are absolutely no incomings and still a hell of a lot of outgoings.

It was encouraging at the Big Show to find so many people who seemed genuinely interested in the service but since then I haven't heard a peep. And I guess it should tell me something about my business model when I have to cast around for friends to take Boy Two for my radio stint rather than employing a rentamummy (basically the whole purpose for which it was set up). It comes to something when you can't afford your own product!

I'm pondering this and many others of life's mysteries in Waitrose café when my mobile goes. It's the Nervous Mum saying if I could do it, she'd really be grateful to have my help one day next week. Suppressing the urge to whoop out loud I make like I'm checking through next week's hectic schedule looking for gaps:

'Um, Monday's not great and Thursday's tricky but Tuesday or Wednesday could work. Any preference?'

(Of course I have absolutely zip on next week and even if I did I'd drop it like a hot rock in favour of something that pays real money, but it never does to seem too keen.)

'Well, the sooner you could get here, the better. I'm a bit at the end of my tether.'

'Tuesday, then?'

'Tuesday it is. Thank you so much.'

Bless her, she sounds like she really could do with some help. I do hope I can give it.

I'm buoyed up by the prospect of some real cash heading for the family coffers and the fact that Boy Two has managed to channel at least half of his baby mush into his mouth instead of just his hair, my hair, the floor and all over innocent bystanders. I positively skip back to Anzac Mum's place. This is not advisable with a baby strapped to your back and it would explain why Boy Two throws up orange goo all down my neck on arrival. Happily the vomit also masks the smell of milky poo leaking from Anzac Mum's baby's nappy so when she retrieves her daughter from the pram she is immediately covered in ooze, necessitating two changes of outfit (her plus baby) and a whole set of sheets for the pram.

Return baby to mother covered in sewage. Good going, doula lady.

On the way home Producer Man texts me with homework for tomorrow's show with Henry (and still there's no pay!). He wants me to watch gory forensic show *Silent Witness*, so we can talk about it on air. This is no great hardship as I find one of the pathologists rather tasty. Apprising Producer Man of this fact I discover that apparently Henry does too. I do hope it's not the same one.

Thursday 2 October 2008

And so begins my mammoth tour of the countryside just to get both children taken care of before I go on air at 10 am. Boy One isn't such a problem. The Very Capable Childminder always collects him from the house at 9 am on Thursdays which saves a run round to her house. I relish my late morning pickup because once he goes to 'big school', he'll go every day of the week. The government pays for five sessions at preschool which I choose to use for three mornings and two afternoons. I can get a better run up at doing some work that way, rather than having five morning only slots. I realised when Boy One was only doing half days at the start that the two and a half hour sessions left barely enough time to take him there and get the shopping in before I had to turn around and collect him. However it only leaves me 30 minutes to deposit Boy Two with Other Mother of Boys. She lives five miles to the west of me, the radio station is five miles to the east. Once I've negotiated a couple of demon one-way systems I'm easily clocking a 15-mile round trip from the house to the Beeb. Since Producer Man has guaranteed that my slot will now definitely be every Thursday I suppose I could make some more permanent arrangements to have Boy Two taken care of 'professionally' (sounds ominous...!). But the Very Capable Childminder still doesn't have space for a baby and there's the small matter of money involved – since the Beeb doesn't pay me, paying for childcare puts yet more strain on already stretched resources.

As I burn past tractors and watch the 'fuel required' light flash impatiently at me, I muse that good ol' Auntie Beeb is getting a pretty good deal out of me. They've got me doing homework, chasing my own tail round the countryside, a cast of thousands (OK, a couple) performing childcare duties and I'm single-handedly burning up the European Diesel Lake. I realise that, working for myself, it's only ever my time and expenses that I'm wasting instead of the corporate shilling. Most time–motion consultants would be horrified at the amount of time and energy expended on 'non-profitable activity'. But I'm having fun and, as a great believer in karma, I feel that surely *something* is going to fall in my lap because of this?

Returning home after an amusing but financially pointless hour on the radio I start hunting through the attic for things to sell at the local Nearly New Sale this weekend. I muse that if rentamummy is as dead in the water as I think it is, and if doulaing fails to take off, I could always just sell everything we possess. Judging by the junk mountain, I reckon it could keep us in nappies for at least six months.

Friday 3 October 2008

I have had a glimpse of the future and it is neither bright nor orange. It is filled with bring and buy sales, doing good works and surrounding myself with items that smell faintly of old-lady wee.

Or at least this is what it will be like if I allow myself to slide from one-time career woman, through half-hearted homeworking and into the living death that is the lady who lunches and 'does good works'.

But today I'm headed for the Nearly New Sale because

we've got quite a hoard of baby stuff in the attic that we can get rid of. Apparently the average house has around £1,500-worth of 'stuff' lying around that could be sold for a profit. So I dust, wash, wipe and wrap a plethora of brightly coloured plastic in readiness for readies. This is an excellent opportunity to sell off some of the noisier, more irritating toys that Boy One seems to have a hard time letting go of. Being a charity they think they can get away with charging a ludicrous commission but a 30 per cent hit on the proceeds isn't too hard to swallow once I see that I can now actually turn around in the attic without knocking over yet another pile of baby-gros and sippy cups.

Entirely not out of a sense of community spirit and wholly because I want to make as much money as I can, I also always offer to help. Of course I am therefore viewed as a wonderfully selfless person (this may or may not be wild speculation on my part), but more importantly I can make sure that my items are always perched right on the top of the pile and thus first to be grabbed in the inevitable melee once the great unwashed public are let in and collectively spy a bargain. Let's just add mercenary merchandiser to my list of talents.

To me, this is only an annual event and therefore bearable. However this year, for some reason, spending the afternoon preparing the hall has given me a glimpse of what my future might hold. There are women for whom arranging the local bake sale or charity do is the highlight of their week or month. They are in their element, bustling around and bossing everyone else about. They pride themselves on their 'good works' and point out that such-and-such organisation *simply* couldn't function without them. In fact were they to be laid up in bed with a cold the world may very well cease to turn. In my apocalyptic vision of the future there is also a lot of tweed involved.

I return home, pour myself a large glass of something at least 13 per cent proof and vow to attack my enterprises with renewed vim and vigour next Monday, 9 am. I may even wear high heels.

Saturday 4 October 2008

The Husband takes Boy One to another swimming lesson. I have only been at one so far. This is so I can get to the sale early to help set up.

Before it starts the helpers are given a chance to shop. I have decided that this is purely a money-making enterprise and I am in no way allowed to shop. To this end, I have come unequipped with any cash or cheques. Until … what's this in my pocket? Fifteen quid? Oh bugger it.

And before I know it a baby-chair harness, Spiderman kiddie computer and talking Woody from *Toy Story* have all leaped into a clear plastic bag and are looking at me accusingly. I keep waiting for the Woody to utter: 'Whatcha waitin' for pardner? Cash machines aplenty hereabouts.'

However, in the final analysis, I do make a profit of £98. I am particularly chuffed by the sale of Boy One's rocking crib. It drove me mad when Boy One was a newborn. Every night he'd shift his weight just slightly away from dead centre and – boink! – slide to one side with his face pressed up against the decorative but painfully knobbly bars. Thus would begin the first of many night wakings. But painful sleeping positions aside, I am even more pleased to sell it because of the mark-up. I sell it for a tenner when I had in fact bought it in the first place from the rag and bone man at the council tip for £3.50. Classy!

Sunday 5 October 2008

The children are climbing the walls at home so I shoo them out of the door with the Husband for a long-overdue trip to the park. I don't do parks. I don't object to fresh air and exercise – fully aired and exhausted children are a thing of joy when they pass out at 7.05 pm. It's the heart in mouth, imagined visits to A&E with dislocated shoulders, skin flayed from faces and leg bones shattered in a million inventive ways that keeps me away. I simply cannot watch four-year-olds cavort around on monkey bars without chewing my nails down to the knuckles. The Husband however is fully appreciative of the boys-will-be-boys dynamic and possesses the male gene that makes fathers oblivious to the danger lurking around every corner that is so blindingly obvious to mothers. He is the perfect person to perform park duty.

I make some lame excuse about needing to sort out our tax

position and dispatch the Husband with orders not to return for at least two hours. He is very happy with this state of affairs as a tax position is something he would consult the Kama Sutra for.

His job requires a good grasp of maths and statistics, but confront him with a bank statement and all the blood drains from his face. When he opened our last mortgage statement he came tearing upstairs screaming: 'Why are we being charged £700? How many times did you forget to pay?' His blood pressure returned to normal when I pointed out that was the interest on a £150,000 mortgage, perfectly reasonable, and we have in fact been paying this – and often more besides – for at least the last five years.

Children finally scarved and hatted and sent on their way, I slump onto the sofa with little or no intention of doing anything about the tax at all. That is until Moira Stuart comes on and ruins my afternoon by pointing out that this year's return must be completed by 31 October or the Chancellor will come round and personally excise his pound of flesh. In my case he's welcome to at least two, which would save all the hassle of trying to get rid of it the hard way.

Sunday afternoon telly being the intellectual desert that it is, I heave myself over to the desk with a sigh and begin to sort through receipts looking for tax-deductible expenses. This is not the satisfying activity it once was. While I was taking the corporate shilling I still sifted through the receipts even though, along with them being tax deductible, for the most part I actually got back all the money I'd spent on expenses. Most of the time. There was one occasion when Human Resources did find a two-hour sushi binge with a so-called client a little hard to swallow.

But the only carrot dangled in front of the DIY accountant is that, being self-employed, your expenses will be offset against the extra amount you need to pay the government. The money itself is long gone. It's something I have trouble reminding myself about every time I leap upon a new laptop or fancy stationery. 'Tax deductible' no longer means 'free money'. Boo.

I tot up all the outgoings in the rentamummy camp and arrive at the following:

Outgoings

Leaflets	£100
The Big Show	£150
Activities for the Big Show	£25
Balloons	£100
Helium	£100
Website	£30
Illustrations	£40
Adverts in local paper for Big Show	£100
Total	**£645**

Incomings

Mrs X 3 hrs 4 September	£40*

Introductory offer, no booking or membership charge, and therefore no actual money for me!

Weeell … the expenses are thoroughly tax deductible all right. Unfortunately they are also extremely salary deductible and lifestyle deductible. And none of the money above even includes the amount of time and energy spent setting it up, the times Boy Two was sent to join his brother at the Very Capable Childminder's on the odd occasion when she'd have space so I could get some peace and quiet, or indeed the multiple admissions to the playbarn so I could get the Husband and children out of the house at weekends. This really isn't going anywhere, is it?

With it down there in black and white it is hard to avoid the fact that I have few options left. I had a couple of weeks of maternity pay left over that came through in September's accounts (a measly £200!) so, aside from child benefit, if I don't return to work it is likely to be the last injection of cash full stop. Is it time to stop playing around?

I can do one of two things. Either I can give it all up as a learning experience, trot off back to the old job while looking around for another place to hang my hat that might pay more/cost less to go to. Or, the alternative is to really pull my socks up and get on with heavy promotion, networking and drumming up business.

There is also, however, a third way. On Tuesday I'll have my first proper doula client. And they pay significantly more for what appears to be less input all round. As a business concept it is also quite a bit more recession-proof than ad hoc babysitting and party arranging. Mind you, so far the figures on the doula front aren't that impressive either:

Outgoings

Leaflets	£100
Website	£30
Training	£400
Total	**£530**

Incomings

Baby Y 5 hrs x £10 p/h	£50

Still, I think there might be more of a future in ladies' fannies than party bags. But do I cut my losses with rentamummy completely? It's not as if it's something I have to actively close down ... perhaps I'll just leave it be and it'll gently fade into the background. Time to focus on getting me some more babies.

Monday 1 October 2008

If there was ever a reason to get off my backside and leave the house, I've just seen it on Channel Five:

'I was married for fourteen years but living a lie. I wanted to be a woman so I cut off my bits.'

And the worst thing is, I can't help looking at her/him and thinking: 'Ooh, not a bad wig – a bit plastic Barbie maybe – but hasn't s/he got the hang of doing her/his lippy!'

I really need to get out and do some more work.

Tuesday 7 October 2008

Typical. Just when I decide to do one thing, the whole lot gets turned on its head again. I spent all of yesterday handing out yet more doula leaflets. I've had a couple of enquiries from the first bunch but, as I said, they get taken, used as shopping lists, forgotten. So, it's back to traipsing round doctors' surgeries, health clinics, cafés, libraries – anywhere that will take these flaming fliers. I get home all filled with renewed enthusiasm for the job then two things happen:

1. Boy Two comes down with some horrendous lurgy and puts paid to the idea that I'll be looking after my doula client today. First day on the first job and I blow her out with about 20 minutes' notice, how professional! I feel doubly bad because the baby's mother is obviously really hoping that I can do something to sort her problems out (and frankly, my dear, so am I because so far I have no real evidence that I'm any good at what I say I do!). She has posted on her social networking page: 'Don't worry, baby, help is on its way!' No pressure there, then.

2. I'm surprised in the middle of updating the doula website by one of the Scary Posh Mummies. She wants a rentamummy. Agh – what do I do? Go the whole hog and say that I've folded it, or go ahead and take the job, which may be just the tip of the iceberg? I decide to

take the job but of course by now all the ladies I'd got interested in being rentamummies probably think it's all gone tits up and will have lost interest.

Scary Posh Mummy says she needs someone for the following night, which is true to the rentamummy remit of emergency cover wherever, whenever. I fudge the issue of other mummies by saying I'll check the duty roster (?) but that I'm pretty sure the only one available that night is actually going to be me. Seeing as I blurted out that the total cost would be £24 for three hours it may as well be, as I've just done myself out of the membership and booking fee for the second time running.

Mother from Work calls for a chat about the dreaded 'going back'. We still know that neither of us plans to go back to the office but even though we keep saying it to each other, it still seems hard to believe. I know I've been moaning that it wouldn't be worth it if you factor in the travel and childcare costs but it would get me out of the house and keep me away from daytime TV nightmares. Plus, I could still go to mortgage companies and tick the 'employed' and 'salary' boxes.

But, but, but … I know I'm earning hardly anything at the moment and I know that in the middle of this so-called credit crunch when we're supposed to be guarding every last penny as though our lives depended on it, my outgoings are exceeding my incomings roughly five-fold. But … even if I earn just a fiver more a month than if I were going out to work, isn't it worth it?

All Grown Up

Now, from spending rather a lot of time achieving not very much at all, I have two jobs on one day. I have to doula during daylight hours and then come screaming home to get the boys bathed and presentable for the Husband before charging back out of the door with my rentamummy hat on. It never rains …

Wednesday 8 October 2008

So finally we get to the first real doula job. I'm not ashamed to admit that I'm a bit nervous. I've done the training – but that seems like months ago now – and I've read the books. Hell, I've even written about babies often enough. But writing is one thing, doing quite another. You know that saying: 'Those who can do, those who can't – teach'? Well, let's add on: 'and those who can neither do nor teach spend all day looking stuff up on Wikipedia so they can write about it.'

Cribbing notes off the internet is easy, but knowing why someone's newborn baby won't sleep just by looking at them is actually quite difficult. Plus, I haven't the heart to tell my client – whose biggest baby issues are sleeping and eating – that Boy One ate nothing but scrambled eggs for two months as I couldn't get him to eat anything else without him making himself sick. I probably also shouldn't mention that Boy Two, now a healthy hearty nine months old, refuses to sleep anywhere but in our bed with his jaws and both hands clamped firmly to my bosom, resulting in permanently chapped nipples and deep-set sleep-deprivation.

We start off well. I am on time (tick), presentable (tick), and haven't yet sworn or dropped the baby. Within the first hour we even make great progress with one of her major problems which is getting her baby to nap without being held. She makes all the usual new-mum noises: 'It's my fault, I've spoilt her ...' Well, how you spoil a newborn baby is beyond me. It's not like she has her own expense account at the sweetie shop.

Having reassured her that there is no such thing as 'fault' and that she'd have to go some to 'spoil' her daughter at this early stage, we quickly discover the root cause of her problem. Nervous Mum is highly intelligent, logical and cares deeply about her baby. She is therefore doomed from the start. She has read too many books, tried to make fact from theory and become confused and frightened by too much advice. This has led her to be so terrified of cot death and so aware of the associated advice that you must keep your baby cool, that she is trying to get her to sleep in a cold room in autumn wearing nothing but a vest. The poor wee mite is blue!

We spend the next couple of hours getting Nervous Mum to trust the evidence of her own eyes ('She can't be hungry, it's not three o'clock yet', 'Is she crying?', 'Yes', 'Is she gnawing at her fists?', 'Yes', 'Is she trying to chew your shoulder off?', 'Yes', 'Can she tell the time yet?', 'No', 'Then she's telling you, "Bugger three o'clock, I'm hungry now, woman, and I'm not going to belt up unless you stick a boob in my mouth"'). It's all going swimmingly.

I even seem to pass the health professional test, which isn't one I was expecting to come up against so early on. The health visitor turns up to weigh the baby and check on mum's well-being. She launches into all sorts of questions and I try to answer as if I have the benefit of years of experience, instead of just what I've figured out since 9.30 this morning. She doesn't turn round to my client and say, 'You've found a right one here!', so things are looking positive.

Before I know it, the day is over and my first job complete. A few slip-ups here and there. The training says you should never offer advice and yet I find myself saying 'I'd advise ...' every other minute. You're also told never to talk about your own children and yet I qualify the advice with 'When my son was little ...' But I think I've got away with it. She even pays me in cash, which comes in very handy, particularly when I go home via the Very Capable Childminder and hand over 80 per cent of it for looking after Boy Two on top of the usual fees for Boy One I suspect that after tax and diesel I have made enough to cover a first-class stamp but it's good experience and Nervous Mum claims to have been so happy with my services that she promises to spread the word far and wide.

Children collected from the Very Capable Childminder, I realise I have just under an hour to scour the supermarket for something for their supper, get it home, defrost it (What am I? Perfect Mother?), feed them, pyjama them and locate a toothbrush. I'm relying on the Husband getting in on time so

I can make my rentamummy appointment. It's the first one (although my client doesn't know that) that I've done and I'm determined I'm not going to be late for it.

So, of course, I am. The Husband fails to get his usual train and rocks up 20 minutes late so I practically drop-kick Boy Two into his arms as I run out of the door. I'm still almost on course for being on time provided I don't get lost. Scary Posh Mummy did point out that the house was a little tricky to find but it's near one of my favourite walking paths so I thought how hard can it be?

Quite hard is the answer. I forgot to take into account the fact that the area looks pretty different when approached by road rather than the right-of-way paths across fields. It's also a bit more challenging in the pitch-black – her area of town being more properly rural, street lights are therefore viewed as an unnecessary extravagance. A few near misses in the Multipla later and miraculously I'm only ten minutes late in the end. Blaming a non-existent tractor for my woes I bustle in and try to resemble the no-nonsense Mary Poppins-like figure she was hoping for.

I also get a vision of my own parenting inadequacies. For a start her youngest daughter is the same age as Boy Two – nine months. While mine screams like a banshee every time I leave the room and insists upon being carried for at least 75 per cent of the day, this little girl is happily feeding herself her bottle on the top landing while her mother tends to her older sister downstairs. Scary Posh Mummy introduces me to the baby and plops her down in her cot, wishes her 'nighty-night', turns off the light and closes the door. Not a peep.

Were this my child there would have been about half an hour of wailing and gnashing of teeth before I gave up and stuck a bosom in the screaming hole. Once he had gorged himself to sleep at last I would have begun a series of complicated and excruciatingly slow movements to manoeuvre myself out of the sofa, up the stairs and – hovering over the sides of the cot – lower him ever so slowly onto the mattress, where I would hold him for five minutes, imperceptibly loosening my grip until he was fully down. This whole palaver usually takes at least an hour and a half and is rarely a guarantee of peaceful sleep, as he wakes at least four more times during the night for a little snack. Is it any wonder the child is in 18-month trousers?

Marvelling at this most placid baby, I go downstairs to my main charge, the three-year-old. Again, this is a most well-adjusted young lady. Propped neatly on a footstool clutching her cuddly she's sparklingly clean and smells of talc. Boy One may emerge clean from the bath but in the intervening period between towelling dry and climbing into bed, he somehow acquires smears and smudges all over his face and hands.

She is informed by her mother that she is allowed another five minutes of *Teletubbies* and then it is one story and lights out. She nods solemnly and before I know it, Scary Posh Mummy is off into the night. If that were Boy One there would be instant meltdown, only resolvable by generous applications of chocolate and inappropriate action films.

I enjoy a peaceful evening in her very lovely home and, as there's nothing on the telly, I think again about how to get rentamummy working properly. This is the second time that I've given out the service for free – not counting the actual babysitting rate, but then that was only going to make me money if I did the job myself. Then I hit on an idea.

We could have two streams of business. One, where the old model didn't change – £15 per quarter membership and £3.50 booking fee. This would be most appropriate for heavy users. But then I could have another stream based on pay-as-you-go mobile phones. Everyone knows that it's not economical to have a pay-as-you-go mobile if you're going to use it a lot, but it's more attractive than a contract if you just want it for emergencies.

That's how rentamummy could operate. A higher hourly rate, say £11 per hour instead of £8 but no membership or booking fee. That way, the rentamummy doing the work gets her £8 an hour and I still get the £3 per hour difference for setting the whole thing up in the first place.

Seeing as Scary Posh Mummy's children are angelic and sleeping soundly, I crack open the laptop and get started then and there updating the website and contact details. I also finally remove Partner in Crime's photo because, effectively, she hasn't been part of the business since ... basically since it started. The irony is that having gone back to work after maternity leave, she was told two weeks later that they were making her redundant. This is not a bad thing. I've never seen anyone so happy to lose their job in my whole life and she got a nice little golden goodbye. However she now has all the spare time in the world to be a rentamummy.

And she's also given me an idea of how to manage the dreaded returning-to-work conversation that's coming up for me in the next few weeks. For whom the bell tolls …

Thursday 9 October 2008

Once again I'm on my mega tour of the county to offload the boys on a selection of carers before making my way to the BBC. Perhaps I should organise something more permanent in terms of childcare for Boy Two. After all, it would give me some definite work hours and an incentive to get more clients in. The choice then would be: pay the Very Capable Childminder or eat. I doubt I could afford to do both (although failing to afford the latter would eliminate the joey pouch without having to pay for a slimming club).

But still I'm beginning to think that if I really want to get the businesses properly off the ground and make some serious money I need to make some real arrangements for Boy Two. It's all very well saying that I can work around him, but realistically? I couldn't have done yesterday's job with him there, for example. I need to be able to focus on these women rather than saying 'Just hang on a sec while I untangle my son from your satellite box – now what was that about postnatal depression?'

I never really entertained the bucolic idyll that working for myself at home would mean putting in a couple of hours here and there while the children gambolled around my feet. I knew it wouldn't all be sipping ice-cold Chardonnay in front of the *Midsomer Murders* matinee. But I did think that maybe by now I'd have a fair idea of how much I'd have to work and when. I'd thought that I could maybe start Boy Two in daycare for a gentle two afternoons a week. But most of all I'd thought a few cheques would be rolling in with reasonable regularity by now. As it stands we're practically getting by on child benefit and whatever change I can find down the back of the sofa.

It's Other Mother of Boys' turn to look after Boy Two while I waffle over the airwaves and I've promised to pay her in kind so swing by Starbucks on the way past. On the latte index of payment in kind it'd probably be cheaper paying for a real childminder though (two venti lattes £5.90, two skinny blueberry muffins £3.40, two chocolate coins for our respective Boy Ones (sorry Boy Two – babies are too young for treaties!), £1 and an OJ for them to share, £1.70. Starbucks' charge for two hours of childcare: £12; childminder cost: £10.00, not counting the diesel required for the 15-mile trip out of my way to get Boy Two to Other Mother of Boys in the first place.

On this occasion I also have to suffer the return-to-work conversation, as Other Mother of Boys is on the last fortnight of her maternity leave. Naturally I commiserate as the thought of returning to three days a week as a wage slave is still anathema, but from my position of relative poverty it's hard to sympathise with her protestations that it's going to be hard to survive on the pay cut she's taking for going back part-time.

Lacking any sense of shame I point out that her pay cut is actually my entire full-time salary, and since working part-time myself after the birth of Boy One that worked out at about £16,000 per annum. Valuable and demanding work though it is, it grates to realise that your top whack achieved after years of experience and training is on a par with that of the teenager who frothed your latte five minutes ago.

I am NOT feeling charitable when she bemoans the fact that she doesn't feel she can afford a new work outfit from Jaeger and that Monsoon might just have to do. I remind myself that my £5 no-brand jeans from the supermarket are a steal and that as they are label-less and have just the right amount of baby sick and scuffing at the heel, I could pass them off as vintage from Camden market. I try not to think of the number of Bangladeshi children who went blind doing the pocket detailing for 5p a day.

Things look up when I get home to find two separate emails enquiring about rentamummy. One is for a party and the other is for a morning's cover for a lady who brunches. I farm the party out to Academic Mother, who bears these sorts of things and is desperate for something to do at the weekends other than listen to her partner bang on about the state of the housing market (not a great time to be an estate agent, then), even if it does involve a church hall and 30 spoilt six-year-olds high on double dip. The other I take for myself because it would be stupid to pass up the money when I've got the time to do it.

Both the new clients have taken the new pricing structure – compulsory three-hour stint for the higher £11 rate. Hopefully they'll think the service is so good that they'll keep coming back and maybe sign up. If absolutely everyone paid the £11 rate then in the final analysis I probably would make more money in the long run but it wouldn't take much for someone else to undercut me and I wouldn't have any guaranteed income in the long term. Gyms excepted, if you sign up to a service you do tend to use it. It does make me think, though. If I'd set the prices like this earlier, would I have had more clients sooner? I didn't get it that badly wrong, did I?

Friday 10 October 2008

For the first time in what seems like weeks I have nowhere to be and nothing – much – to do. Obviously I have websites that could do with updating, contacts to make, leaflets to distribute and I could always take Boy Two to one of the toddler groups and try to hassle people there about renta-mummy or the doula service. But, other than working, I don't really have much to do. Just how I like it.

And it stays like that for all of an hour and a half until the Glamazon turns up at the door with an invite to her daughter's birthday party. She intended just to push it through the door but I'm feeling starved of adult company these days so she's barely made it to the front gate before I yank open the door to call after her.

Agreeing to come in for a cup of tea, she gingerly steps over that morning's detritus. Why is it that every time I tidy no one darkens my door for days but as soon as the living-room floor is covered in toys, half-chewed breakfast, stains of dubious origin and at least two nappies that have yet to make it to the dustbin, I get company. Well, on this occasion I suppose it is my fault as I invited the Glamazon in, but I acted before I had time to turn on the shame centres of my brain. It's just as well both rentamummy and the doula thing are designed for me to take my work elsewhere. I don't think my living room – which could sometimes be a borderline case for public health services – is a great advert.

We shoot the breeze for a bit and then she asks how the doula job went.

'Really well, I thought. I felt hugely underqualified at the start but it didn't take long to get in the groove. I thought I did an OK job in the end. The client certainly seemed happy,' I answer.

'So, do you think it's something you really could make a go of?' she asks.

'Hope so. I've left it a bit late to change my mind now!' I laugh, aware that there's more than a little ring of truth in that.

'I know we talked about doing something a while back – kind of got left by the wayside for a bit – but if you think it's going to work then I'm really tempted to go ahead myself,' she admits.

'Ooh, competition!' I joke. 'But seriously, that would be great. Remember, I was always keen to try to team up somehow. Two heads better than one and all that.'

'I've got to do something, there's just no money coming in any more. But I'm still worried about what you do with the kids. If you can't tell when you're going to work, how are you going to deal with childcare?'

'It's true it's a bit of a quandary but I think I've got a plan.'

'Do tell.'

'Well, I think I'll keep putting Boy Two in with the Very Capable Childminder, whenever she has space but hopefully he'll take over Boy One's slot when he goes to school for the full five days. That means I've definitely got Wednesday, Thursday and Friday covered. I can schedule any postnatal stuff for then and if a birth does come along then I'm just going to have to wing it. Of course, if you and I were to work together then I'm sure we could work something out between us… . Why don't we work together?'

I secretly hope she'll agree because, despite saying to the contrary, I absolutely cannot afford to put Boy Two in with the childminder either. If we worked together then at least we could look after each other's kids and save ourselves the cost.

'Let's do it!' the Glamazon announces suddenly and

reaches into her bag for some paper and a pen. 'Right, let's get me on this course first and then we can get going. Give us the details, then!'

After the abortive attempt with Partner in Crime all those months ago it feels good to have someone else to talk turkey with. That's the problem with working for yourself. You only have yourself to talk to, yourself to delegate to and, if it all goes wrong, yourself to blame. And you're pretty shit company if you want to go to the pub and get drunk after work.

I pack the Glamazon off to get her daughter, arming her with doula textbooks and course details. This, of course, is going to make my tax calculations even more of a headache if we set up a partnership. I barely understand the whole sole-trader deal, let alone anything else. But it feels good to know that I'm not flying totally solo any more.

A new partnership Reading doula, more clients for renta-mummy just when it looked like it was going to go to the wall. It's all looking up.

Tuesday 14 October 2008

I'm up to my elbows in old smelly mattresses, garden junk and wine bottles at the municipal tip when I get a text from Producer Man:

'Research pussy galore. Uv got to do Roger Moore on Thursday.'

Struggling past the double entendres (and bypassing the

fact that he's mixed up his Connerys with his Moores just so he can be rude) it dawns on me that I'm going to interview double-oh-seven in two days. Now, fair enough, it's not the current double-oh (he can come and give me some secret service any day, and I dare say he looks significantly better in a pair of Speedos than the now-octogenarian Mr Moore), but come on … it's the SAINT! It's the EYEBROWS! It's a proper godshonest sleb and I get to interview him. I'm not sure the man next to me expects a loud, throaty 'GET IN THERE!' when he is offloading his hardcore, but it is quite hard to hide my delight.

I sit in the car inhaling the heady scent of decomposing household waste, alcohol-soaked bottle banks and leaking paint tins while I call just about everyone I know. My Luddite Stepmonster even promises to find an internet somewhere so he can listen on the Beeb's website, so this must be a major coup! Who knew that going to the dump could be so much fun?

Wednesday 15 October 2008

The Glamazon calls to tell me that she's signed up for the next available course to become a doula. So now, even though the Partner in Crime is no longer my partner in crime, I have a new partner in crime – and not in the business I originally started with the original partner in crime. Best laid plans, eh?

The Glamazon insists she's only going to take on the post-natal doula part as the thought of all those lady bits is making her feel quite ill. From my limited experience thus far, it's looking as though that's where the money is anyway so it shouldn't be a problem.

rentamummy is picking up and it looks like there may be life in the old doula yet. This doesn't mean that I'm anywhere close to making enough money to live on yet, though. I send out a couple of writing pitches to some magazine contacts but I'm not holding out much hope. They haven't heard from me in ages and may well have moved on. Even if they did commission something, it would be months before I got paid. But it never hurts to try.

To bolster the finances I start looking around on the internet to score some free samples of washing powder and baby wipes (if you can't earn any money then you might at least try to get as much stuff as you can for free). I must have signed up to a few 'fill in questionnaire for vouchers' places, though, as the amount of spam in my inbox has trebled overnight.

However, as is the way with the wild, weird world of Google I end up at a market research website.

This market research company isn't offering any freebies, but it is offering real money for jobs done as mystery shoppers. I quite fancy myself as one of those.

I fill in their eligibility questionnaire and find that I am indeed eligible. Mind you, what I thought might have been a bit of a laugh starts to look like basic training for MI6. You have to read all these briefings about what constitutes a greeting versus an acknowledgement. When it is right to prompt and when it is not? How often you are likely to be required to use your own money to purchase? Do you use your real name or lie?

Here was me thinking this was just wandering into a shop to see whether the person behind the cash register looked at you as if you were pond life or not, and if there were enough size 12s on the rack (there never are – is there a size 12 black hole somewhere?). Instead I have to undergo briefings and tests to determine whether I might have a particular staff bias or if I understand how to be subjective versus objective.

It's all a bit daunting to start with but once you get past all the pseudo-secret-service language it seems quite straightforward. The research company is quite honest and points out that you are unlikely to become rich doing this – the average fee is £12–15 per assignment and you don't often get more than one or two a week. It's not going to keep me in the manner to which I'd like to become accustomed but it's not bad all the same.

Thursday 16 October 2008

I've been silenced! Well, temporarily at least.

I've been telling everyone about my big moment on the radio today. The Husband has been instructed to sort out the live streaming recording thingy on the computer to make sure the interview is captured for posterity as what could be the defining moment of a broadcasting career.

As I arrive at the station, Producer Man hands me my

briefing sheet and I'm good to go with lots of pithy questions to put to the man with the most mobile eyebrows in showbiz. And then Henry says: 'Put the headphones on if you want to listen in …' while simultaneously turning off my microphone and piling into the interview. So I won't be doing any talking, I take it?

After the show I slink back to collect Boy Two and field emails and calls. 'Did I get the wrong time?' one asks. 'You were very … quiet,' says another. Not interviewing Old Rog was one thing, I can live with the disappointment, but it was mortifying having to tell everyone that I didn't actually do anything in the end. And to add insult to injury, *Blue Peter*'s Peter Purves was on after him and I didn't get to ask him anything either. I had a doozy about sticky-back plastic lined up to ask him.

(I'm ashamed to admit that it took until I was 27 to realise that sticky-back plastic is in fact Sellotape, but the BBC isn't allowed to use brand names because of advertising. My mum always said that I couldn't do the 'make and dos' that they had on the show because it was so hard to find sticky-back plastic anywhere. I think she actually didn't want me to pour a full bottle of Fairy down the sink just so I could make Dougal from *Magic Roundabout*.)

Friday 17 October 2008

After my almost day of sloth last Friday, I book myself into my own diary and take what the Americans call a 'personal day'. Bum around doing nothing much other than allowing daytime television to slowly reduce what's left of my brain to primordial ooze. I think this is finally achieved some time around one of those auction programmes where everyone does a teeny tiny little sex wee when they discover that Great Aunt Vi's horrendous vase might make all of twenty quid at auction.

When I was in the office I used to daydream about Duvet Days (the UK's altogether more honest version of a personal day, which to me sounds like you're going to get your wobbly bits on the wrong end of a speculum). I'd think, 'If I worked from home I could just knock off whenever I felt like it. I could just get up one morning and think, "Stuff this, I'm going shopping."' But instead I'm now so busy with the 101 things I need to do to keep body and soul together, plus I'm attacked by the raging guilts when I cease to be productive, convinced that the moment I choose to flop on the sofa will be the one someone tries to make a doula booking on that internet form that I just haven't got around to fixing yet.

Saturday 18 October 2008

I have gone from a moment of purest inaction, to a moment of great hyperactivity. As usual, Boy Two gets me up at stupid o'clock and as I am lying in bed being dozily munched by the small I start thinking about all the little jobs that need doing around the house. 'Must put up that coat hook' sort of thing.

Unfortunately, in the intervening period between 5 am and the relatively humane 6.30 am, daydreaming has escalated into a full-blown plan. As soon as I can rouse the Husband from his slumber I dump the baby on him and shoot off downstairs, calling out: 'Look after him, I've got some tidying to do!'

Said tidying involves digging up the whole of the front garden, including several buckets of gravel, a rampant nasturtium, umpteen bulbs of indeterminate origin and a hyacinth that appears to have wrapped itself around the foundations of the house. All before 9 am.

Boy One gets in on the act, deliriously happy to be involved in sanctioned wanton destruction, and soon we are both covered from head to foot in mud. I've spent so long tied to a computer, planning world domination, that I've begun to forget the simple pleasures of mucking about (in this case, literally) with the kids. I've even begun to see spending time with them as an unwelcome distraction from business chores that I need to be getting on with. And isn't that the point of this whole exercise? To be able to spend time with the boys without feeling stressed, tired and cranky? I make a mental note to spend more time in a mud hole in the garden and less time hotwired to the worldwide web.

Now with a blank canvas to play with I hotfoot it down to the garden centre leaving the Husband with solemn promises not to spend more than thirty quid on a few petunias. Returning an hour later with about £150-worth of Cotswold stone and white chippings I set to work again. The Husband is a little suspicious that I managed to grab such a bargain down the shops ('Fifty quid for that lot? Are you sure?'). I'm sure my skill with creative accounting will come in very handy with my first real encounter with the taxman – which reminds me, ugh …

Several hours, tonnes of mud, sand and artfully arranged stones later I am done. Muscles are aching, the jeans are so muddy they are beyond rescuing and the children have done for the Husband once and for all. Everyone is piled in and out of baths, gobbles a plateful of macaroni cheese, and one by one we begin to snooze on the sofa.

Finally hoisting the snoring children upstairs I fold myself up on the sofa with an excessively large glass of wine and even bigger sense of satisfaction. I haven't had such a sense of well-being in weeks, all from lugging a few flagstones around. To be fair, I really used to love gardening. Before the boys came along I'd be out in the back until all hours.

Even when I was heavily pregnant with Boy One I'd be shifting great lumps of sod around, although you're not supposed to. Something to do with cat pee making babies grow three heads or something. Whatever it was, like runny eggs and blue cheese, I wasn't going to give up playing in muddy puddles just because I was pregnant, so I got the Husband to liberate a few latex gloves from his lab. I figured that if they provide a good barrier against powerful carcino-genic chemicals, they'd withstand a bit of cat pee.

But while I was pregnant with Boy Two it was mostly during summer and I couldn't take the horse-pill-sized antihistamines to deal with the pollen so I had to stay indoors and watch while the garden turned into the outdoor equivalent of Miss Havisham's parlour. Then, once he was born, we seemed to slide into all the palaver of rentamummy and doulaing courses and there just never seemed to be the time.

Come to think of it, this whole maternity leave has been marked by a total lack of time. After I had Boy One I don't think one week went by that didn't see me, Other Mother of Boys, Academic Mother and the ex-Partner in Crime planted out back with a glass of Chardonnay in one hand and a spoon of baby mush in the other, getting pleasantly fuzzy by 4 pm. I can count on the fingers of one hand the number of times I've made it 'out to play' this summer, thrashing rain and howling wind of the average British summer notwithstanding.

I used to spend every other day taking the train to a new park, or strapping the baby to my back and the walking boots to my feet and yomping over hill and dale as a way to pass the hours and melt off the joey pouch at the same time. It worked a treat too, and I got a demon tan. I've only managed to go for one walk like that with Boy Two and even then I found myself having to run back towards the end as I remembered I'd promised to do a talk about doulaing to a local postnatal group.

Getting off the treadmill was supposed to enhance my quality of life and slow it down. Instead, I seem to be running furiously just to be able to stand still. Have I made a big mistake?

Monday 20 October 2008

An article in the *Daily Mail* online makes me sneeze tea out of my nose this morning and it's a real bugger to get it off the computer screen.

Infamous for its eternally confused view of the nation's women, the paper comes up with some fantastically contradictory features. It can tell women that they're all going to be obese couch potatoes with a drink problem by 2012 on page 6, and then flags up a report on page 23 that women should drink more red wine if they're to improve heart health. Things like that.

So it isn't with high hopes that I start reading an article about 'Portfolio Woman'. However, I am a bit startled to discover that I actually agree with it.

In essence, it suggests that today's modern woman (who, in the *Daily Mail*'s mind, is one who is graciously allowed three hours a day away from the Aga to perform charitable works and perhaps even do a little light typing) gets by having not just one main job, but many smaller ones – a portfolio of employment so to speak.

It really strikes a chord because until now I've just thought that I was being completely random, directionless and unfocused by not being able to decide which avenue to take. Should I be a rentamummy? Should I go back to writing? Is doulaing for me? Instead, according to this article, what I should be doing is all of them. I should be keeping one eye on rentamummy while I hire out my services as a doula and then I should be writing about it all in *The Times* in the evening. Plus, every now and again I should be doing a spot of mystery shopping and running the odd Baby Yoga class. Crikey, the *Daily Mail* has captured the zeitgeist! Whatever next?

Mind you, it is when I read to the end of the article that the nasal propulsion of camellia-infused chai (sneezing tea) occurs. I quote:

> Around the core, like satellites, the Portfolio Woman usually tries to win a couple of non-executive director-ships, which take up less time and are pro rata more lucrative. Most require a monthly board meeting, plus membership of a sub-committee. Private-sector boards do, of course, require knowledge and experience of busi-ness and are filled by headhunters, so you have to do the rounds. You must have done a senior executive job in a company or equivalent.

Oh. The only board I have knowledge of is the Monopoly one and I always seem to land on Park Lane once the hotels are up. As for committees, I think I've inadvertently got myself installed on the one for pre-school but, as they spend most of their time trying to get me to work for free, or stinging me for money for new paintbrushes, I can't see how they're going to contribute to the mumpreneur portfolio coffers.

The author of the piece handily put down a few bullet points for us potential portfolio women to follow. I think they need clarification – for the real world.

Top tips for portfolio working:

- Put yourself about. Visit headhunters.

Put yourself about indeed. Turn up at anything where you think you might be likely to make money. Be aware that you will most probably have one or more small children with you who will try to undermine your professionalism by a) doing a stealth poo and revealing a neck-to-ankle skid mark only when a potential client picks them up for a cuddle – the client will naturally be wearing dry-clean-only cashmere at this point, and b) commiting a minor felony (older children biting another child, bearing their bottom, belting a sibling) but immediately, on catching your eye, screaming with terror, 'Don't smack me, don't smack me, I'm scared when you smack me!' and collapsing quivering with fear in a sobbing heap at your feet.

- Think hard about the time commitment – each part-time job takes longer than you think.

To a mother this does not even bear mentioning. By the time our children are a few months old we are well aware that it can take up to half an hour to leave the house for the supermarket because the child poos and requires a full change of clothes, then pukes and requires another change and then the family poltergeist hides all the wipes/nappies/car keys. However you will also have newly acquired skills that allow you to have yourself ready to go out in three seconds flat. This is all the time you have to yourself all day and you now no longer care that you only manage to brush your hair once a week. You have now become an avid collector of hats.

- Don't be too snotty about taking up offers, particularly in a new field.

When the maternity pay runs out and you've bought value bread for the sixth week running, a tenner for some babysitting looks like a king's ransom. If someone offered you your old hourly rate you'd pass out from the generosity.

- Find an office away from home.

Home is not the problem, it's the children. An office more than 5 metres away from children is a boon and it will soon become acceptable to surf the Wi-Fi from your toilet seat while glueing the children to a *Scooby Doo* marathon downstairs. Stair gates are child-proof until they're at least four years old.

- Invest in a BlackBerry.

This is false. You don't need any more technology than you already have. The children will only drool in it or drop it in the toilet. Spend the £300 instead on catering packs of chocolate, toy cars and Barbie dolls for buying silence. Your children will be hell to live with by the time they're five but by then they're the school's problem.

Saturday 25 October 2008

With the boys safely deposited in the gym crèche and the Husband steadfastly pounding away on the treadmill, I make my escape and don my superhero identity: Mystery Shopper Woman! I contemplate flinging my pashmina over my shoulders like a cape before realising that I haven't run down the street shouting, 'Deh-neh-nur-neh-nur-nur, deh-neh-nur-neh-nur-nur,' since I was seven and wore a hooded parka to school. I remind myself that I'm a grown-up and narrowly avoid looking a complete berk. I've got a 'gig' round the corner from the gym, checking out if a local bank branch is behaving 'on message'. My mission, should I choose to accept it (it's £12 for ten minutes' shopping – well, dur …), is to go in and ask about switching bank accounts. So glamorous.

All goes well until our man with the ISAs sends me on my way with a cheery goodbye and a fist full of leaflets. In the best *Family Fortunes* tradition: En–Errr! You were supposed to take my contact details, mister. You needed to offer me an appointment. I'm supposed to feel LOVED!

And so I set off back to the gym café to fill out my questionnaire, input my results on their website and claim my £12. Kerching! I used to get so much admiration from the gym staff about my dedication – until about four months ago I'd be there at least four times a week and I would actually be doing some exercise.

But since the whole 'let's work for ourselves' fandango I've still been going, but basically only to use the café computers and almost-free childcare. Arm curls have been limited to lifting lattes and dunking biscotti. Which would explain the stubborn reluctance of the joey pouch to shift and the ever-increasing circumference of my arse.

Mulling over the choice between a skinny latte or diet coke (former, calorific but basically meal in itself; latter, virtuous but leaves wiggle room for small to medium muffin – a dilemma), in my daze I all but run over one of my old (or current?) workmates.

'Hey, you! What are you doing out here in the sticks?' I cry, genuinely chuffed to see him again after all this time.

'We live here now. Came down to be close to the missus' dad,' he replies, looking equally astonished and, gratifyingly, pleased to see me in unusual surroundings.

'So you're not at the mag any more, then?'

'Oh I am, I just commute from here. You must be due to go back soon, surely?' he asks.

'Not due back until mid-December, but I've got to let them know one way or the other in about three weeks,' I reply, realising that it's the first time since the usual bitching to Mother from Work or the Husband that I've said this out loud.

'One way or the other? There's still some debate?' he asks. I can't have been radiating enthusiasm.

'Well, you of all people now realise what the commute is like,' I answer. 'And now that I've got two ankle-biters – my fault, I know – it's going to cost me to go back. And you know more than anyone how unlikely any form of pay rise is going to be.'

'Mmm, blood and stones come to mind. So you really don't think you'll be back?' he presses.

I'm torn between the desire to prattle on and on about the multiple plans for the family empire, and a sense that revealing my hand to someone who works closely with the Editrix might not be the brightest thing to do, however sweet my friend is.

'Hard to tell, still haven't made my mind up,' I waffle, noncommittally. Then I have a flash of inspiration. 'Tell me, gorgeous –' (flattery, I hope, will lube his indiscretion) – 'what with all the crunch and recession and whatnot, is the company looking a little … wobbly … at the moment? I mean, they've gone public so the shareholders are going to be looking for some major money savings to protect their dividends. What's the redundancy situation looking like?'

'Couldn't tell you, I'm afraid. I know that there have been some jobs going but there doesn't seem to be a pattern, and I think your lot look safe.' He shoots me a puzzled look so

I'm obviously failing to conceal my hopes for a juicy redundancy package – an added bonus when you think I am already 75 per cent convinced that I won't be going back anyway. I try to look worried.

'I guess they won't appreciate me coming back and bumping up the salary bill again,' I say, angling for more info.

'Hard to tell, but if you're after some redundancy money it can't hurt to ask. Wouldn't bank on it, though.' Damn. Rumbled.

Monday 27 October 2008

I message the Editrix confirming our coffee date for 12 November. We're meeting Mother from Work as well for a general catch-up but I know the 'other' request is there: Please make up your bloody mind about coming back.

I ask if I can arrive a little before Mother from Work so that we can have a confidential discussion about 'work-related issues' and the Editrix agrees. In a little over three weeks I will have half an hour to plead my case. Now, to figure out a way of making the idea of paying me to go away sound very attractive (I wouldn't have thought it was that hard, to be honest).

Today is also the first day of the parenting challenge that is half-term. I know that my ultimate aim is to be able to spend more time at home with my children, but I don't necessarily mean that to be all day, every day. Coming from the extreme of seeing my offspring on Wednesday morning and then again on Saturday morning, a couple more hours a day would have been idea. A full 24 seems a lot like hard work. All I say is, be careful what you wish for.

To dilute the brain-atrophying, all-day cartoon marathon I invite one of Boy One's friends over for a playdate. I don't know the little man's mother very well but she's Russian and I'm itching for the opportunity to try out some of my excessively rusty vocab on her.

Installed in Boy One's bedroom, Mumushka and I small talk a bit while the kids get used to playing outside the normal pre-school surroundings. I've made this playdate thing part of a concerted anti-bullying campaign. I figure that if you have all of your kids' friends round to play all the time, they know each other too well – and hopefully get on too well – to end up as bully and bullied. It's my insurance policy against one of my worst fears as a parent, second only to the idea that it might be Boy One who is the bully.

Mind you, with the need for catering packs of fish fingers, party rings and blackcurrant squash, it's turning out to be quite an expensive insurance policy. Perhaps I should just save up for bodyguards.

Not that Mumushka will ever need bodyguards for her kidski. Russians are notorious for being, frankly, hard as nails. It's all that kidnapping, corruption and communism that they've had to put up with. Mumushka is a gentle sort but I suspect there is a vein of steel in there somewhere.

Mumushka is already divorced from kidski's father. It

always surprises me to discover that Boy One's friends' parents are separated. My own parents' fractured relationships – four weddings and, yes, a funeral between them to date – has left me under no illusion about the fallibility of the married state but it still shocks me when a) my peers and b) people with young children split. Mind you, since Boy Two's birth, I have fantasised about flinging the Husband's belongings onto the street from an upstairs window more than once, accompanied by instructions to sling his hook and never darken our door again. Except in my fantasy I only have custody of beautifully behaved children who use up all their bad manners and backchat at his house.

As a struggling single parent, though, Mumushka is quite an inspiration. She holds down a part-time job in the village to keep the family solvent, while retraining to be a photographer in her spare time. I've heard some good things about her pictures from friends in the area and decide that, seeing as it's about time Boys One and Two had a joint portrait done, I'll get her to do the deed. Help from one mumpreneur to another kind of thing. Although it's unlikely that she'll need the services of a postnatal doula any time soon.

Checking my email while the boys chow down on their pasta pesto – Boy One is pushing it around the plate and Boy Two is throwing it at the curtains with surprising accuracy – I discover another rentamummy request. A childminder has gone down with something nasty and the mum needs cover for

Thursday and Friday mornings of half-term. Again, she's going with the pay-as-you-go option, but who am I to complain?

Unfortunately it's not free money for me as I can't do either day. I've got the radio on Thursday and my own Very Capable Childminder has dropped me in it for the Friday. Academic Mother is out of the question as she actually does academic things on Thursdays, having been made a permanent if poorly paid – member of staff some time ago. The Glamazon would have stepped into the breach but she has just gone and got herself a stop-gap job as a receptionist at the local dentist's every Friday so she's out. Sharing the job between her and Academic Mother may have worked but I don't think it looks too organised and I'm still enthusiastic enough not to want to give a bad impression.

However, it's looking like I'm dangerously short of mummies to do my bidding. Don't tell me that the moment this looks like it might evolve into a going concern I haven't got the resources to keep it going? A round of frantic emails and voice messages later and the ex-Partner in Crime helps out yet again. Newly unemployed she's quite happy to play dollies with a seven-year-old girl and her four-year-old brother for a couple of hours. She admits that her one-year-old will probably be glad of the company as his twin four-year-old cousins are away on half-term holiday and he misses having someone to play dinosaurs with. Not sure how the seven-year-old girl will feel about dinosaurs versus *High School Musical* but I'm sure they'll get on fine. And it's more money in the kitty!

Tuesday 28 October 2008

Day two of the half-term hell-idays. Naturally it's tipping down with rain, the local playbarn is full to the rafters and both urchins are driving me up the wall before 9 am. There is only one solution in times like this – shop.

Feeling flush from the rentamummying and doulaing for Nervous Mum, I pack the kids into the car and head for Ikea. It may not be the first place you think of for peace and respite from two energetic boys but it's surprisingly effective.

For a start, you can be the parent from hell and they still won't kick you out if your trolley is full. This means Boy One can jump on as many beds and sofas as he likes (which he is naturally not allowed to do at home) and spin in the cheapo office chairs until he's sick if he wants to. It's not my carpet that will need cleaning.

Boy Two can also rampage relatively unfettered through the children's display, disgorging Swedish felt toys from storage cabinets all over the floor and rearranging the lighting shelf.

Once they've had their fill of wanton destruction I repair to the front of the shop where you can 'check in' any child over three for 90 minutes' free childcare.

I availed myself of their services about 14 months ago when I was last here but I hope they haven't kept records. At the time I just wanted to get on with the shopping and wasn't interested in torturing the furnishings or the assistants. But Boy One was just a couple of months too young. As he is tall for his age and a precocious sort I thought I'd get away with making him over three, but I didn't count on my total lack of maths skills.

Unlike lying about my own age, which comes as second nature much of the time, it's not as simple as lopping off a year or two (hard to explain why the almost three-year-old is actually one, if you see what I mean). So I had to think of a month that would make him over three but not by so much as to be unrealistic. They develop so fast at that age that claiming he was too old would make him look a bit thick, and too young could make him a candidate for Mensa.

Birth date revised by a safe five months I pottered off into the shop. Shopping took 15 minutes, including sourcing the obligatory 100-pack of tea lights and unnecessary lazy Susan and photo frames; it was the cup of tea and cake that took the other hour. Returning to fetch Boy One at the allotted time I was asked to verify I had the right child by confirming his date of birth. Now this I often get wrong even when I don't have to fib, because he was born the day after the Stepmonster's birthday so I often confuse 24 September with 25 September. However I now had the added confusion of having to remember which month I'd used. The pause between the childminder asking the question and my answer must have been mighty suspicious, as must have been my reply, which wasn't so much 'Twenty-fifth May' as 'Twenty-fifth May?'. But eventually I was allowed my own son back. So even though I can now legitimately plonk him in the crèche I wonder if they keep the record card that I filled in last time. Does this mean that I am going to have to make up a whole new identity this time?

Boy One safely ensconced, minus the third degree, I trot round the shop with Boy Two in a trolley. I've come here for the usual odds and sods (tea lights again) but also a new mattress. Our old one has lasted since before we were married but with the addition of two children, three house moves and goodness knows what other abuse, it has comprehensively had it. Flush to the tune of about £200 from Nervous Mum, rentamummy and the odd mystery shop (I'm not counting my expenses right now!) I'm determined to treat myself to a new one.

The Husband objects, of course, on the basis that our mattress is perfectly good (i.e. he's not actively being stabbed by springs in the middle of the night; but I haven't the heart to tell him that I was so tight-fisted when we bought that one that it wasn't sprung in the first place) and that we can't afford it. Well, the latter argument has never held much sway with me anyway and, possessed of a credit card, which is the same as free money, I have the means, motivation and muscles to lever a new mattress into the car, with or without his help.

Help, however, is something that I really could do with right now. So that my arms wouldn't drop off in the Sisyphean exercise that is trying to navigate Ikea's 'marketplace', I've stuffed Boy Two in a trolley. But this is an ordinary supermarket trolley designed to contain tea lights and lazy Susans, not a queen-size sprung mattress. So I have to find the industrial-type trolley too.

Gingerly driving both my trolleys through the aisles of glassware stacked high especially for me, I eventually make it to the mattress storage place. I can lever one off the top of the pile but can I get it onto the empty trolley? Every time I get more than a corner on the base the trolley shoots off in one direction or the other. I can steady it with my foot but if I try to hold onto it with one hand the mattress then threatens to catapult off the pile and crush me or Boy Two or both.

Wedging everything together temporarily I head off to find a lemon shirt that signals a member of staff who might be willing to help. Two strapping lads head my way and I waylay them.

'Could you help me? I'm having trouble getting a mattress down.'

Both shrug and reluctantly follow me to where I've parked Boy Two.

'Not got anyone with you?' one asks.

'No, the Husband's at work. Can't see how a single mum could manage this on her own, though!'

'Oooh,' the other sucks his teeth. 'You don't do Ikea on your own, love. You need some help.'

I stop short of reminding him that's what he's there for and instead start tugging away at the mattress, hoping that the fear of mattress squishage will galvanise them into action. After much huffing it's on the trolley and I wiggle both child and furniture towards the tills, before running back to the crèche drop-off to collect Boy One. Boy Two is left parked underneath some frighteningly early Christmas decorations and I hope no one decides that the Swedes have gone for realism with the Baby Jesus this year (or in Ikea-speak: BabJesik) and picks him up along with the impulse-buy mini Daim bars and ice-cube trays for the knock down price of £11.

Puchases purchased, children loaded into the Multipla, I begin the task of getting the mattress in the back. The checkout girl looked at me with disbelief when I said I wasn't getting it delivered (at £40 – are you crazy!) but was going to drive it home myself. I have great faith in the Multipla.

Besides, I'd got the old mattress home from the same place in the back of a teeny Polo. How hard could it be? Well, quite hard, as it turns out. For a start the last mattress was thin and cheap so folded with relative ease into the back. This one is all thick and padded and isn't for bending. I huff and I puff and bribe Boy One with disco music and Daim bars, and after 20 minutes' hard labour it is eventually in. Unfortunately so is the trolley it is perched on and it takes another ten minutes of tugging to get it out from being wedged under the back bumper.

As the kids doze on the way home in the car I reflect on the latest insane project and come to the conclusion that I've got a bit of a habit of shooting off and doing mad things on my own. Landscaping the front garden (consequence: livid bruises all up and down arms); redesigning the bedroom, knocking down shower cubicle using dumbbell bar at 7 months pregnant (consequence: pelvic dysfunction and inability to get up from sitting on the floor without having to crawl on all fours for five minutes first); repainting all the wood in the house overnight (consequence: gloss paint in hair, hall carpet requiring replacement at cost of £1,450) – all my mad projects that I decide to take up on a whim.

What's the lesson here? That I'm pretty good when I branch out on my own? Well, yes. But equally, because I refuse to allow anyone to help and so I almost always go off half cocked, the end result is reasonable but often left unfinished and could have been done better (the shower still leaks one year on and the mattress is filthy from being rubbed against the bumper and car tyres in my struggle).

I've been doing well enough getting the story out there about rentamummy and the doula service, but I've got lots of leaflets left here sitting doing nothing, the website could do with an update and I've got a list of tasks on my to-do list that are never going to get to-done. If the Glamazon comes on board then perhaps that's just what I need to keep me focused and on track. That it's great to have someone to bitch to about work is by the by.

Thursday 30 October 2008

On my way to the radio stint I follow the latest news in the furore that TV presenter Jonathan Ross has caused by being rude to Manuel from *Fawlty Towers* (the actor Andrew Sachs). It seems he and his co-presenter Russell Brand left lots of rude messages on the actor's answer phone about his granddaughter's preferences for the horizontal samba. Brand jumped before he was pushed and Ross has just been suspended for three months without pay, which, based on his £13 million salary, should save them a couple of hundred thousand over the £1 million mark. Does this mean that they've got enough money to start paying me for all this now?

Halfway through the show the regular Financial Whizz comes in. I think we're discussing inheritance tax today. Not something I've had the good fortune to have to deal with. Not that no one's died – my relatives have chosen to drop like flies. It's just that, in keeping with family tradition, we're all as poor as church mice so tax is not an issue.

During one of the songs, Financial Whizz updates us on the imminent arrival of his first child. We are about seven weeks from B-Day (I keep telling him that means it's at least nine weeks but he's not having any of it). He's had one antenatal class with his wife so far and, to put not too fine a point on it, he's bricking it. Half-jokingly I offer my services but make a mental note to poke him incessantly about it on Facebook until he gives in. Could my first baby be due?

Friday 31 October 2008

Today is the cut-off day for sending back those dreaded tax

returns and can't you just tell as Moira gurns out at me from every daytime ad break. By the way, why are you talking to us? If we need to be filling out tax returns then surely we're all beavering away earning money and not watching *Cash in the car booty attic* all day. Perhaps there are more people like me out there who try to squeeze in five minutes of work between a heavy schedule of daytime telly and internet surfage?

Anyway, due to the government's customary efficiency I haven't been sent a tax return. I have got a bill for the National Insurance payments that I opted out of several months ago, but no tax return. It's not the end of the world, as the deadline for doing it online isn't until 31 January and that's how I would have done it anyway (at midnight on 30 January, probably). But I get a sense of righteous indignation any time someone demands money with menaces then can't be bothered to put the bill in the post.

I also get a very interesting writing proposition that is something I hadn't thought of doing for a while because I've been so busy starting all these mumpreneur things. It's a ghost-writing job for a 1960s starlet. It sounds really interesting and it could be good money for basically being a hired typist with a reasonable grasp of grammar. Then I find out that they want me in central London this afternoon to meet her.

Now, I've promised Boy One that we can go trick or treating. As a Scot with a good work ethic the whole idea of trick or treating makes my blood run cold. It's not the going round getting sweeties – that's fine. I just think you should have to earn them. In Scotland we call it guising and you have to recite a poem, do a trick or sing a song. How valued these little turns are when five youths turn up on your doorstep and you have to stand there in the freezing cold listening to an off-key rendition of 'Supertrooper' while you're missing *EastEnders* and your tea's going cold, I'm not sure. But it's a damn sight better than threatening to egg the begonias if you don't get enough Mr Chewits in your tuck bag.

So I have the option: go to London and chat up an early 1960s icon with the potential to make money into five figures, or take Spiderman and a pumpkin (Boy Two, not an actual squash) to frighten some sweets out of an old lady or three.

The pumpkin wins hands down.

Monday 3 November 2008

A message pops up on my Facebook from Nervous Mum, whose baby I'd helped last month. Clicking it open, I'm anticipating the next challenge – reflux? Won't sleep? Weaning issues?

Instead there is gushing praise – which is good – about me being a great baby teacher. She goes on to say that because she's been so boosted, her three-month-old baby is now happily settling in her cot and doesn't sleep in bed with mum any more. It's great to know that even from my first job I seem to have cracked it, and that's how it should be, but it's not so good that she now doesn't need a follow-up (and paying) visit.

It's not all doom and gloom though, as she thinks one of her baby-group friends is looking for a doula, and for a longer term than she needed me, which is good news. It's all very well doing jobs for £50 a day, but I'd much rather have a regular client who needs me for £30 a morning, three days a week. She thanks me again and promises to put her friend my way. I make a mental note not to be so damn good next time!

Wednesday 5 November 2008

True to her word, Nervous Mum's friend calls. Her own parents and in-laws all live abroad and she's finding it difficult having little support. It's a typical scenario in these parts. Being plumb in the centre of the commuter valley for London we're all close enough to work there (including me) but for most of us it means leaving home at 7 am and not getting back until 8 pm. For a new mum at home alone with a colicky baby it's no fun.

I offer to go round to see her tomorrow evening to see how I can help. I'm not relishing the idea of colic, which tends to make a baby cry non-stop for three hours every evening, but at least I will be able to hand it back when it's time to go home! I'd better brush up on my burping technique.

Like Nervous Mum before her, she sounds ever so grateful that I'm coming over, which in turn makes me pretty nervous. With the business that I've chosen to set up I feel more than a bit responsible. It's not like I'm making cupcakes for a living. The worst that can happen there is they won't rise or you get the wrong shade of pastel pink (don't think food poisoning – you'd really have to go some to poison someone with a cupcake). Being a doula, these women – and men – and their babies are really depending on you. It may not be life or death (though you have to watch what you recommend around cot-death guidelines), but how you perform can have a big impact on the whole family's welfare. It's not just about the money.

Thursday 1 November 2008

As I wait to hear from my new client, I set about pestering the Financial Whizz on his imminent arrival. While last week we were having a bit of a joke and a banter about it, this week he looks altogether more serious. I ask what's changed:

'We had another antenatal class,' he answers.

'And so?' I ask.

'Well, the first one was all about what to do when labour goes to plan – all that back-rubbing, juice-drinking, brow-mopping and whatnot. Last night's was all about what goes on when it doesn't go to plan, and how often that happens,' he replies.

'How often did they say?' I ask.

'Frighteningly often,' he replies.

He goes on to say that he doesn't think he's going to be very good with what he calls 'women's stuff'. Not that he's an unreconstructed male chauvinist or anything, he is just, quite understandably, terrified of the truck that's about to be driven through his wife's lady parts, and also displaying a startling amount of self-awareness when he admits that, by and large, 27-year-old men are not generally well equipped to be midwifery assistants. While I suspect the hand-holding he's after may be as much for him as it is for me, I tell him to check out the website so he understands what doulas do, and to get hold of me if he thinks he might want help.

Tuesday 11 November 2008

The Husband and I sit down after a chaotic day. Tomorrow I've got a date with the Editrix and I honestly don't know what I'm going to say.

'I thought you were dead set on not going back?' says the Husband.

'I wasn't … I am … I mean, I really don't want to go back. We can't afford it for me to go back,' I reply, before adding: 'But it's the real deal. Once I go there and say, "I'm not coming back," that's it. I'm unemployed. I've quit a perfectly good job at a time when the whole world is plunging headlong into recession. Am I mad?'

'Would it be that difficult for you to get another job, if push came to shove?' he asks.

'Probably not, though whether it's the career-defining, Pulitzer-prize-winning editorial post is another matter. But, fundamentally, there's always Waitrose down the road,' I joke, only not really.

'What are you most worried about, then?' he asks.

Good question. Am I worried about identity? What's wrong with working at Waitrose? It pays the same as my editorial job did. But I fought so long to be able to put 'journalist and writer' in the occupation box, am I ready to give that up? What do I put instead? Doula, childminder, mumpreneur …? What if I want to be all that and more? Is that just greedy?

But is there any reason I can't take on all of those roles and many more besides? I may have laughed at that woman who wrote about the portfolio women – the ones who simply couldn't decide which executive board to serve on, when the reality was more about which pre-school committee versus Saturday job to take up. Is there any reason I can't be a doula and write at the same time (apart from the need for sleep, but I'm rapidly learning that sleep is for wimps – and it's probably not what we want to hear, but us mums and Maggie Thatcher have a lot more in common than we might have thought)?

'I'm just worried that I'm going to make a big mistake and telling the Editrix makes it seem so final,' I reply.

'Look, you've made your case for not going back. You know what I'm like about money. If I thought we'd be any better off by you going back to the office I'd make a much bigger fuss about you quitting. I've seen the amount of slog you've put into the last few months. Sure, it's slow, but nothing happens overnight. It's not like you've bought a lorry load of toys you can't shift, so we're not in debt or sleeping under a mountain of unwanted merchandise. If you have to work in Waitrose for a few months to make ends meet then so be it. It's not the end of the world.'

And then he stuns me:

'I'm so proud of what you've done. I actually quite enjoyed all the Saturdays with the kids when you shooed me out of the house. I wouldn't change that, or you, for anything.'

'Even when I said being married to you was like being given a life sentence sharing a cell with a hyperactive three-year-old who couldn't wipe his own arse without a map?' I ask, amazed by what appears to be nothing less than complete unwavering support from the Husband.

'Even then. Besides, that wasn't even your best. Look, you do what you think is right but, from what I can tell, the decision is already made and you're just trying to find a reason not to be the brave, bolshie, beautiful lass I married. Go to town tomorrow, spend too much money on a sandwich, tell the boss where to stick her job and then come home and make us all millionaires. Now, since there has obviously been an invasion of body snatchers who have replaced our children with ones who are actually both asleep at the same time, can we have an early night?'

You know what? It's all good.

Wednesday 12 November 2008

A fraught journey into London to meet the Editrix, which, if I was in any way wavering about the thought of going back to work, convinces me that it's not an option. I'm squashed behind an 80-something chap, immaculately turned out in a business suit, who is, like I was when pregnant all those months ago, completely invisible to all the 20-somethings sitting down nodding their heads silently to their iPods. I've had to bring Boy Two with me – the Editrix would have my guts for garters if she missed out on a baby cuddle. I am therefore discovering another hitherto unexplored talent – I can breastfeed anywhere, absolutely anywhere. On this occasion perched on top of golf clubs in the luggage rack on the 9.33 to London Paddington.

Boy Two and I wander around central London a bit as we're too early for the meeting. The skies are grey, the buildings greyer. I lose count of the number of times we're shoved off the pavement into the road by bustling commuters and tourists. It's a shock to suddenly be invisible again – walking around the centre of our local town I can't get anywhere in five minutes as old ladies stop to coo at the baby and acquaintances hang back for a quick chat.

We arrive at the café that was picked for our meeting and I have to say it's nice to be somewhere where the ratio of buggies to people is less than one to one. The Editrix bustles in, designer jeans free of yoghurt stains, hair brushed, make-up done. She dumps an armful of magazines, diaries and envelopes on the seat next to me and scoops up the baby for a cuddle.

'Oooh! That baby SMELL! Yum!' she cries. I haven't the heart to tell her it's probably milk sick and baby wipes that she's getting. I'm not altogether averse to it myself.

She deposits the baby and I'm the next one in line for a squeeze and a slobber.

'So good to see you! You've lost weight!' she exclaims, lying through her teeth but the compliment is no less welcome for it.

We settle down, burble through the usual small talk – who's doing what to whom, who left under a cloud and who's been promoted – before the inevitable pregnant pause ensues.

'Honey,' I begin, 'I think I should tell you …'

14 November 2008

Dear Editrix

It is with regret that I write to inform you that I will not be returning to my post after this period of maternity leave and I offer you my resignation as Associate Editor.

I choose to do this for a number of reasons. As I'm sure you noticed in the last year or so of my employment, it was getting harder and harder to leave my little boy in the morning, knowing I probably wouldn't see him again until the next day. It often inconvenienced you as much as it did me when I called at 7 am to announce that I wouldn't be in on press day because of the snots/runs/rashes that frequently visit small people without warning.

Also, you are no doubt aware that journalism is one of the lower-paid professions. It is now a profession that, officially, cannot sustain a family with two children! Much as I enjoyed your company, the thought of effectively paying to come to work was a tough hurdle to overcome. In the end it proved impossible. But, naturally, should you feel the need to throw any freelance pounds my way, I should be only too happy to accept.

Leaving is a particularly difficult decision to make as this brings to a close more than seven years on the magazine, six of which I have spent working closely with you personally in various capacities. I hugely enjoyed our working partnership. I also enjoyed the socking great Christmas hampers the ad agencies dropped on us, but that's a different matter. It's hard to swallow that I won't be on the receiving end of 2 kg of pick 'n' mix this Christmas.

Beyond the daily grind we had some fun, didn't we? There was the time you frightened off James Bond by waving a pair of lacy blue knickers above your head outside the Dorchester. And when I bent Pierre Cardin's ear for half an hour at 2 am, a little worse for wear from the free cocktails at MTV's Cannes Film Festival party. I don't think my opening gambit went down too well: 'Good lord! I didn't think you were still alive!' And I'm still stunned from being surrounded by Hobbits at a marketing award ceremony.

It's a shame that I won't get to use our brand-spanking-new offices with real daylight and a carpet that doesn't make an audible squelch around the water cooler. I have fond memories of those last few days of pregnancy when Mother from Work and I would use our maternity jumpers to stop us from inhaling the paint fumes coming from the renovations next door.

I hope you keep up the tradition I started of trying to keep plants alive despite the lack of fresh air or natural light. If the worst comes to the worst and the aircon fails, you can use them like a budgie down a coal mine. If the leaves turn brown in less than an hour it may be time to leave!

I'm going to miss the scrum to get ready for our annual office Christmas party, always held in January to save money. And I'll treasure my two awards for being the third best journalist in the company, 2005 and 2007. At least I can say, hand on heart, that I've never been second best...

Our paths may cross professionally in the future, but until then let's remain friends and keep in touch. Particularly if there's any pick 'n' mix going begging. I'm not proud.

Best Wishes

Former Associate Editor

Epilogue

Six months down the line and I still haven't taken back the corporate shilling. Most evenings see me wedged in the corner of the sofa, laptop on knee, trying to block out the latest American mini-series or made-for-TV film as the Husband relaxes after a hard day at the office. I'm still working, fixing webwonks, answering emails, setting up renta-mummy appointments for the next week or reading up on a particularly tricky problem presented by one of my doula clients. If I'm feeling brave I may even update my tax book after January's self-assessment deadline left me a quivering wreck and almost did for the marriage once and for all.

Was it worth it? Yes and no. I still long for the security of the office. Not just financially. Having at least one small child around my feet almost full-time isn't my ideal scenario. I rarely get more than an hour to get on with things at any given point in the day before a nappy needs changing or a school run done. I no longer get the sympathy given to working mums; there is the assumption that I am sitting on my bottom eating cream cakes and watching *This Morning*. In fact, I am working at running a babysitting/party organising service, advertising for doula work and being a part-time webmaster – all on top of a full-time job as childminder, cook, cleaner and family admin service.

Financially we are about as poorly off as it is possible to be without both of us being unemployed. I earn barely anything yet am not entitled to benefits as I am, quote, 'unavailable for work'. Unavailable? I'm very available, there's just no one available to pay me. The complex system of family, working and childcare tax benefits baffles me but, as far as I can understand, the Husband earns just enough for us to be ineligible for all but the most basic child benefit.

However, we are in the early stages. If a business does not actually fail in the first year, it still usually fails to turn a profit in the first two. After that, if you do everything you can to keep going, it can begin to take care of itself. I am lucky. I have few overheads and no stock or premises to worry about. It's just me, my ladies and my creaky old laptop. If the worst comes to the worst and we have to give up the broadband I can just relocate to the local caff and, for the price of a latte, steal their Wi-Fi.

Now, instead of scraping my backside out of bed at an ungodly 6 am, to pack lunches, shoe bags, nappy bags, handbags and laptop bags, I rise at a leisurely 7 am to enjoy Coco Pops with my boys. I'm at the school gate to drop off and pick up (most days) and revel in the gossip, or possible business leads, that I glean from other mums. I've even almost, sort of, joined the committee.

Though it's probably an extravagance we can ill afford, I'm back at the gym trying to work off 'computer bottom: an enlarging of the glutes caused by prolonged periods of inactivity in front of a keyboard, combined with close proximity to sources of food including fridge, freezer and M&S petrol stations'. It gives you a bit of that skipping-school feeling to plough up and down an empty pool at 11 am, knowing that, about now, friends and ex-colleagues are deleting their fifth penis-extension offer of the day. I may even be getting a bit thinner, which is a good thing – they say that thin people earn more money. 'They' don't say how but who am I to question it? Now, pass the celery …

Even the marriage has weathered the storm, though it isn't without its sticky bits. Nothing to do with the business, it was that bloody birthday cake that almost killed it off! I've learned to be kinder to the Husband and if that means not spending his money on spontaneous trips to Gap, so be it. I've recognised (but he hasn't) that yes, it is easier to go into an office and let the boss take control. It is easier to get on with work – even if it's challenging, doesn't always go to plan and can sometimes seem utterly pointless and demoralising – if you don't have to go and wipe someone's nose/fingers/ bottom every five minutes.

But I also recognise that it's a huge responsibility to know that your whole family's financial security rests on your shoulders while the wife sorts herself out. That even if you don't want to get up in the morning and go to work, you have to because those three faces that beam at you from the front door as you drag your sorry ass up the road are relying on you. And that can be a burden.

I've been lucky so far in that I've got a network of people who support me and the business. There is Other Mother of Boys who takes in a Jones waif and stray when their mother is too busy to feed them, and the Glamazon who stands as back up if someone decides to give birth in the middle of our family holiday. Rentamummy couldn't exist without Hello Vera, Academic Mother, Pre-School Mum, Partner in Crime and many others who give up their time and their sanity to go and play with other people's kids.

Being a mumpreneur also means being a Jackie of all trades because it seems, in the early days at least, that if you want to make enough money to survive, you have to find it where you can. If that means running a business and a family while taking in ironing or designing websites or even going back to the old job for a bit, then so be it. It may be romantic to be the starving artist in your garret but your children won't thank you for it. Besides, for me the starving has never been the problem, it's the champagne thirst on the grape-juice budget that's been difficult.

Who knows where we'll be in another six months? With Boy One at school full-time by then, we'll be able to afford another place with the Very Capable Childminder. Maybe by then it would be worth going back to the world of nylon trouser suits and CrackBerries? Maybe rentamummy will be heading for the FTSE? Maybe we'll win the lottery and bugger off to a Caribbean island to do stuff-all for the next 50 years. All I know is that tomorrow I have a full day of breathing exercises, Tumble Tots, website repairs and a trip round the park with a three-month-old whose scream can shatter glass, and has already shattered his mother. Note: *that's* multitasking!

Acknowledgements

Though *The Mumpreneur Diaries* is the story of my first year in business, I am but a small player in a cast of thousands without whom none of this would be possible.

To:

Other Mother of Boys, Partner in Crime, Very Capable Childminder, Mother from Work, Editrix, Academic Mum, Glamazon, Anzac Mum, Producer Man, Hello Vera, Mumushka, Pre-School Mum, Celeb Mum and the Outlaws. (You know who you are!)

And of course the Husband, Boy One and Boy Two.

And to those I can name – in no particular order – without fear of reprisal or physical violence:

Dylan J, Rebecca S, Celia H, Lisa D, Sian J, Arnold J, Rebecca D, Ruth M, Gemma C, Nadia S, Antony W, Henry K, Julia W, Marie C, Rachel J, Joanna F, Asya B.

And very importantly to my agent, Jennifer Christie of Graham Maw Christie; to my publisher Laura Kesner and Katherine Patrick and the rest of the team at HarperCollins.

I owe you a huge debt of gratitude and I suspect, several drinks. Much love and many, many thanks.

MJ x

Mosey is a writer and journalist whose expertise spans business to parenting and all points in between. Mum to Boy One and Boy Two, she is frequently frazzled, bemused and knackered. This does not stop her watching bad US drama instead of 'sleeping when baby sleeps' (whoever said that only has one child) or making a start on the washing up. For the latter, she has employed a husband, to whom she is paying minimum wage and even less attention.